Walking in Haunted Gloucestershire

Florence E. Jackson and Gordon Ottewell

Published by Sigma Leisure – an imprint of
Sigma Press, 1 South Oak Lane, Wilmslow, Cheshire SK9 6AR, England.

British Library Cataloguing in Publication Data
A CIP record for this book is available from the British Library.

ISBN: 1-85058-403-6

Typesetting and Design by: Sigma Press, Wilmslow, Cheshire.

Cover picture: Chosen Hill, Glos. (Courtesy of W. and L. Jones)

Printed by: Manchester Free Press

Preface

Gloucestershire is a county outstandingly rich both in scenery and in tales of mystery.

Its scenic appeal – the Cotswolds, the Vale of Severn and the Forest of Dean – has been the subject of countless books, prominent among which is a bewildering range of walking guides. These include books of long-distance walks, pub walks, family walks, railway walks, and many others, all of which serve to increase awareness of the wealth of natural beauty and interest generally to be discovered within the county.

Similarly, Gloucestershire's remarkable reputation for tales of mystery and folklore has long been recognised. This too, had given rise to various books, usually collections of stories which, while whetting the appetite of the reader for more, all too often make no attempt to place the stories in their physical landscape and thus enable the reader to trace the actual locality in which they are set.

In this book, we aim not only to make good this deficiency but to encourage the reader to explore, by means of short circular walks, a number of carefully-chosen locations associated with stories of mystery. The stories themselves, many of which are published here for the first time, have been painstakingly researched, wherever possible through interviews with actual witnesses. They can be read in the usual way, of course, but many readers will, we hope, be prompted to explore the localities in which the incidents described took place.

We hope too that the book will appeal to walkers who seek access to unfamiliar areas of the Gloucestershire countryside – or to some of the county's striking towns – whether or not they are especially interested in mystery and folklore. To this end, the route descriptions are supplemented by notes on the history, wildlife and scenery to be enjoyed on the walks. In other words, our book is intended to fulfil two distinct roles. Whether you use it purely as a source for compelling stories, exclusively as a walking guide, or as a combination of the two, we trust that it will provide you with hours of pleasure and a deeper regard for this wonderful county.

Acknowledgements

We are indebted to all of those people who helped with the writing of this book, and although their names are too numerous to mention we particularly wish to thank all who have told us their stories and allowed them to be used here.

We are also grateful to the hotel keepers and their staff who spared time to open up haunted rooms, to tell of the occurrences reported there, and to provide names of local historians.

For practical help with photography, Mr. Steven Stone's aid was invaluable, as was the assistance of Nita Arnott and Joan Walton who cheerfully took on the tedious task of helping to check proofs.

Florence E Jackson and Gordon Ottewell

Contents

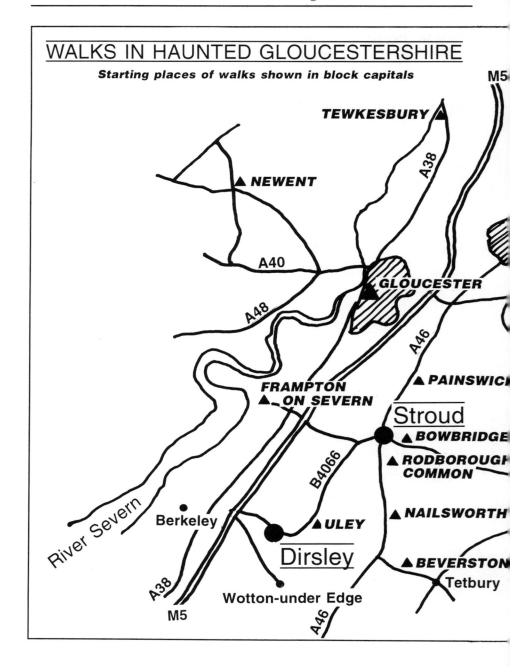

WALKS IN HAUNTED GLOUCESTERSHIRE

Starting places of walks shown in block capitals

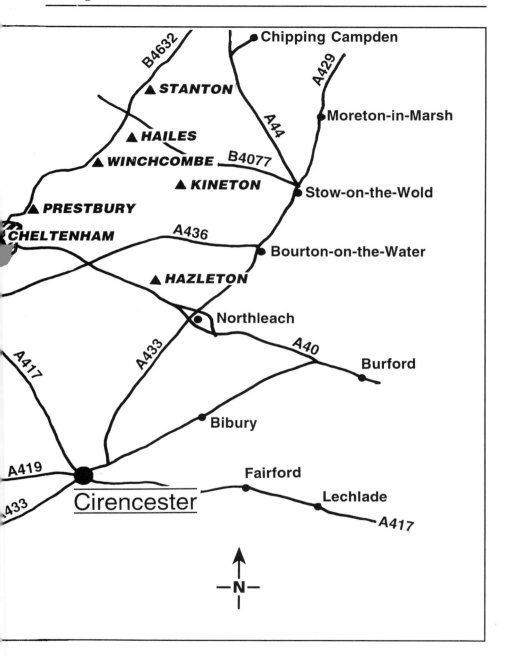

The Municipal Offices, The Promenade, Cheltenham, Gloucestershire

Introduction

There are 17 walks in this collection, ranging in length from just over a mile to almost six miles. They enable you to enjoy some very pleasant parts of Gloucestershire, while learning about the local folklore and visiting well-authenticated haunted sites.

Each walk is preceded by an introductory section which gives you some brief background to the area and describes some of the ghostly happenings which have been reported.

In both the introductions and the walks themselves, haunted sites and the names of ghosts are identified by BLOCK CAPITALS.

Notes about the walks

Generally speaking, the shorter distances tend to apply to town walks. These routes are along pavements and through public parks and are therefore in no way strenuous or subject to the vagaries of the weather. The country walks, by contrast, are routed along a variety of surfaces - minor roads, lanes, tracks, bridleways and field paths. The last two of these categories can be muddy and slippery after rain, and walkers are strongly advised to wear sturdy waterproof footwear, and to allow plenty of time to cover the distance.

Several of the country routes entail climbs. Gloucestershire gradients are comparatively gentle but inexperienced walkers are advised to tackle the easier routes first. Read the notes under the heading 'Terrain' carefully before setting off.

Without exception, the lanes, tracks and field paths covered on the walks are public rights of way. Usually the routes are well-worn, and in the case of bridleways and footpaths, often waymarked. However, such seasonal agricultural activities as ploughing can sometimes temporarily obliterate stretches of some routes. If in doubt, walk round the edge of the field to regain the right of way further on.

Maps

The sketch maps are drawn to a scale of $2^1/_2$ inches to a mile and are intended for use in conjunction with the walk directions. Together, the two are sufficiently detailed to render other maps unnecessary. Even so, walkers will derive more interest from the walks by having the relevant Ordnance Survey sheet available for reference so the map numbers and grid references of starting points are included in the text.

1

PRESTBURY

There is no better place to start looking for ghosts in Gloucestershire than Prestbury, reputed to be the second most haunted village in England. The difficulty is to know where to begin, but perhaps the best place is THE BURGAGE – the oldest street in the village and the scene of many hauntings, especially as all of the stories concerning them have been recounted to me personally.

Prestbury Crossways, where the galloping Cavalier is heard

Halfway along stands PRESTBURY HOUSE, occupied for a short time during the Civil War by Cromwell's men. Knowing that Royalists, camped on Cleeve Hill above the village, were in need of aid and would probably attempt to send a messenger to Gloucester, they stretched a rope across the street. When the Cavalier came galloping through the night his horse stumbled and fell, delivering rider and despatches into enemy hands. Many people living in THE BURGAGE claim to hear the galloping horse, the clatter of stumbling hooves, a short silence, and then the sound of the riderless horse racing into the night.

A skeleton found nearby in the last century is believed to be that of the Cavalier, executed on the spot.

Others living in The Burgage hear the stamping and snorting of horses in the night, and of a light "which goes around the bedroom as if someone is shining a lamp but there is no one to be seen outside". Two sisters who lived near the crossroads where Mill Street joins The Burgage were determined to see the horse they so often heard, and would drop whatever they were doing to dash outside, but they never saw it though they declared they felt it gallop past them.

PRESTBURY HOUSE is now a Hotel but from 1607 until 1964 it was owned by the Capel family. Shortly before the last war when Major Christopher Capel lived there, a Scottish family, visiting Cheltenham, were seeking a pony for their 10-year-old daughter. Hearing there was one for sale at Prestbury House they went one Sunday afternoon to see Major Capel. The pony was admired and discussed and conversation continued in the garden but the child grew bored and wandered off to old stables near the border with Mill Street. As she drew near she was delighted to see people gathered around tables, dressed in clothes like the characters in Jane Austen books. They took no notice of her but she stood there, enjoying their laughter and merriment, then, running back she cried: "Mummy, Mummy come and see the fancy dress party"

At first her mother took no notice, but the child was insistent so, reluctantly, she walked with her towards the stables.

As they drew near even the child could see the party was getting out of hand; there was a noisiness and rowdiness about it, but to her astonishment her mother scolded her. "You're a very naughty girl saying there was a fancy dress party. You shouldn't make up fairy tales like that just to get attention".

The child was punished but insisted she had seen the party and the memory remained though it was thirty years before she again visited Prestbury and research revealed a famous GROTTO existed on that spot in the 18th and early 19th century where "The Nobility, Gentry and Company at Cheltenham may be accommodated with Breakfasts, Dinners and Tea etc. on the shortest notice. Neat Wines etc...". Charles James Fox, and Dr. Jenner were among the visitors, and in 1817 the Duke of Gloucester "with a select party had passed an evening in the Gardens".

But by 1819 it had become an Inn and later the Inn Keeper was fined "for permitting tippling in his house on Sunday".

It became a place of ill repute and was bought by the owner of PRESTBURY HOUSE in 1859 "because it had become noisy, especially at weekends". It was on a Sunday that the "fancy dress party" was seen by the child, who accurately described the fashions of the period and the noisy scene.

On the opposite side of THE BURGAGE is SUNDIAL COTTAGE home of a gentle ghost. No one knows her full story but it is believed a young girl, forbidden to marry the man she loved, was confined to her home where she consoled herself by playing the spinet. On summer evenings, when all is quiet, the gentle sound of music can sometimes be heard wafting along the Burgage. An unlikely tale? Perhaps, but during the last War a mother and her 12 year old son fled from the bombs of London to live at Sundial Cottage.

After a short time the boy became irritable, looked unhappy and was off his food. At last, persistently questioned by his mother, he blurted out, "I can't sleep because I keep hearing funny music"

Puzzled, the mother changed rooms with him. Then she too heard "the funny music". It was only then that she learned of the story of the spinet.

Look again at your map and walk along Tatchley Lane into Deep Street, where you will see the house called THREE QUEENS. An interesting house, the central part dates from the 16th century, the front was added in 1714 and the kitchen wing in 1862. Until recent years it was the vicarage. When the late Canon Urling Smith lived there inexplicable noises were often heard, but no one was alarmed. Visitors were told, "Don't worry; it's only Mrs. Brown." When the vicar's son came home ill from Nigeria, however, he was distressed by the presence, and so "Mrs. Brown" was exorcised, evidently successfully as she is not heard now. On the opposite side of the street is a BUNGALOW, home to the village warden. There, and also in the THATCHED BAKERY glimpses are caught from time to time of a hurrying monk.

The three stone cottages on your left are thought to be the oldest in the village. When a family moved into the MIDDLE ONE a few years ago, the four year old boy refused to be left in the kitchen alone when his mother went upstairs, complaining that he didn't like the soldiers who came in.

"What soldiers?," he was asked. "Funny soldiers with boots up to here," pointing to his thigh, "and with big hats".

He was a newcomer to Prestbury, and too young to know that a Civil War skirmish had taken place outside his home, and that the Thatched House opposite bears the marks of musket fire. Not a bad description of the soldiers though.

The third stone cottage is believed to have been used a a mortuary for the Prior of Llanthony's "cannon's regular," i.e. priests living under rule, and the long garden of REFORM COTTAGE next door was their burial ground. This garden and house are regular haunts of the Black Abbot, seen and heard by many people at Christmas, Easter and All Saints Day.

Shortly before the last war, Mr. and Mrs. Couzens moved in and lived there for many years. They grew accustomed to his visits, but a few years ago, after the death of Mr. Couzens, the house was sold to a couple from London. They told me they soon became aware of "a presence" but were not disturbed by it until they decided to carry out major alterations by putting a floor into a high barn, dividing it into upper and lower rooms. One of the workmen complained that he felt there was "always someone watching him" and he did not like working alone. When the alterations were complete workmen and owner went to the upper room and as they knelt down on the floor, spreading the plans out to check them, a heavy plant, encased in macrame which hung above them swung violently. The plant pot, normally difficult to lift out, crashed to the floor between them.

"You have never seen three men go downstairs so quickly," the owner told me, "We were all very shaken".

It is not at all unusual, however, for ghostly activities to take place when old buildings are altered.

Following your map once more, turn past the telephone box into the churchyard again and St, Mary's church will be facing you. Here the Black Abbot used to walk down the aisle, and although it is believed he was exorcised, that does not prevent him from taking an interest in what goes on around the churchyard and many people claim to have seen him there after funerals. A former vicar once saw a monk sitting on a table top tombstone outside the porch one morning. "As I went over to speak to him," he said, "He faded slowly away in front of my eyes".

As you take the short steps into MILL STREET, opposite The Plough, pause for a moment, for this is a place where the Black Abbot has been seen early in the morning, looking across into what is now the entrance to holiday homes, but was once the farmyard of Church Farm. During the last war a land girl arrived there for work about 6 o'clock one morning, looking pale and frightened, declaring she had seen the Black Abbot on the steps. Perhaps this is the reason why horses, and sometimes dogs, refuse to pass this spot. A former postman, Jock, used to start his rounds very early in the morning when horses from village racing stables were being taken out for exercise. Hearing them coming down MILL STREET he would pull over to the church wall to allow room for them to pass and call a cheery greeting to the stable lads. Sometimes though he heard them coming and trot past, but they were not to be seen and no one answered his greeting.

The Plough, Mill Street

Now, as you make your way back to the car park, via the entrance to Morningside, you may care to walk a little way up there to catch a glimpse of the now derelict MORNINGSIDE HOUSE, where another monk, "with an unpleasant leer" used to slide around the walls of the drawing room, but at IDSALL HOUSE, which overlooks the car park, an attractive woman has been seen brushing her hair in front of a mirror.

Stories are told of many other ghosts in Prestbury, including jockeys, grooms and horses, as would be expected in a village long associated with famous trainers and their stables. And mysterious iron wheels and gruff voices break the silence of NOVERTON LANE about 2 o'clock some mornings. The best known of all Prestbury's ghosts, however, is the BLACK ABBOT who wanders around many parts of the village not described here, for it should be remembered that from the 12th century the Bishop of Hereford's palace was near Spring Lane, (close to Prestbury Park where the Gold Cup is run), whilst later the Prior of Llanthony lived first in Noverton, on the far side of the village and afterwards at The Priory, so no doubt there was much coming and going between these places.

Many who see the Black Abbot express surprise that he looks 'very real', so you may pass him yourself, unaware that you have seen Prestbury's most famous ghost.

The Walk

Route: Prestbury – Queen's Wood – Southam – Prestbury.

Distance: 3$\frac{1}{2}$ miles.

Terrain: Mixture of field paths (wet patches after rain) and pavement walking. Gentle gradients only.

Finding Prestbury: Prestbury lies on the B4632 (Winchcombe road) on the NE edge of Cheltenham. O.S. Landranger Sheet 163 (Cheltenham and Cirencester).

Park and Start: Free car park near war memorial, off B4632. Watch for signs. GR 972239.

The Route

❑ From the car park approach turn right, then right again along Mill Street to reach the B4632.

❑ Turn left along pavement and in about 100 yards, cross to a stile and signpost indicating Cleeve Common and Southam.

❑ Follow the direction of the yellow arrow across a field and cross a stile into a lane.

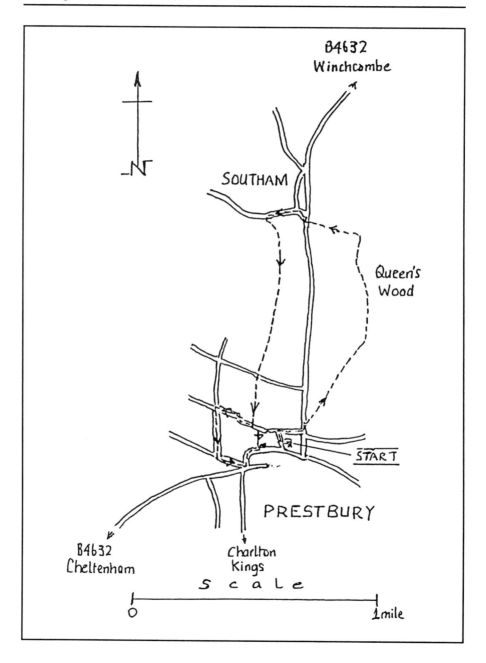

B4632
Winchcombe

SOUTHAM

Queen's
Wood

START

PRESTBURY

B4632
Cheltenham

Charlton
Kings

N

s c a l e

0   1mile

❑ Follow the footpath sign opposite along a track as far as a stile straight ahead at a bend.

❑ Cross a field half right to a stile, beyond which the path forks. Follow the left-hand arrow.

❑ Climb towards Queen's Wood and turn left along its edge to cross a track and reach a stile.

❑ When the woodland sweeps uphill, keep straight on through hawthorn scrub to reach a lane through a handgate.

❑ Turn left down to the B4632. Cross and turn right. Follow the pavement to the left and keep left down Southam Lane.

❑ In about 150 yards, turn left along a footpath signposted Prestbury. Cross a stile and keep left at a fork to follow a well-used path over stiles and through paddocks and fields back to Prestbury.

❑ Cross Shaw Green Lane and pass through handgates to reach Mill Street opposite the church and Little Priory.

❑ Turn right and pass railings on left. Immediately behind the brick pillar at commencement of the wall stood THE GROTTO. Pass the mill on the right, followed by Home Farm, with its interesting group of buildings, to reach a crossroads.

❑ From here a pleasant stroll can be taken along Lake Street opposite, in which are several fine buildings, including a thatched barn.

❑ Retrace steps to the crossroads.

❑ Turn right along THE BURGAGE, the oldest street in the village. In a short distance on the right is SUNDIAL COTTAGE. The dial can be seen on the far gable. On the left is PRESTBURY HOUSE HOTEL.

❑ At the end of The Burgage, turn left into Tatchley Lane, then left again at the busy junction into Deep Street.

❑ Pass the house on your left named THREE QUEENS and a row of THREE STONE COTTAGES.

❑ Immediately beyond the cottages, standing back from the road, is REFORM COTTAGE.

❏ Continue past the pharmacy and at telephone box turn left along narrow footpath at side of King's Arms to enter churchyard.

❏ Turn right in front of ST. MARY'S CHURCH porch and down STEPS into MILL STREET, noticing the thatched Plough Inn on the left.

❏ Turn right, and right, then left and right back to car park. (Notice IDSALL HOUSE overlooking the car park. Behind, and derelict at the time of writing stands MORNINGSIDE HOUSE).

Points of Interest

Prestbury is an ancient place. The skeleton of a Beaker man of late Neolithic, or early Bronze Age, was found, with his beaker, in Mill Lane in 1938, and the village is mentioned in a Charter of 899 A.D. when the Manor belonged to the Bishop of Hereford, as it still did when Domesday Book was written. In the 13th century, the Manor, situated in what is known as Prestbury Park, was "rebuilt of stone and moated around". In 1560 it passed into the hands of Elizabeth I but by 1698 it was dismantled. Traces of the moat can still be found near the bottom of Spring Lane, on land almost adjoining the Race Course, known to thousands today as the scene of Cheltenham Gold Cup.

A smaller Manor, owned by the Prior of Llanthony on another moated site, was occupied from 1250 to 1450, but by the 16th century the Priory, adjacent to the church, had become the Manor of this Prior.

Prestbury was a market town by the 13th century with a weekly market and annual fair held in the Burgage, the oldest and widest street, which lapsed after fire destroyed most buildings on the east side in the reign of Henry VIII.

There was fighting during the Civil War and graves of men from other wars lie in the churchyard. Famous trainers, jockeys and horses have lived in Prestbury, and for 17 years the Queen Mother stopped here on Gold Cup day. Fred Archer the jockey "ate his first porridge" at the King's Arms, and Charlie Parker, who played cricket for England and took 3,278 wickets, was born here. Families with the ancient names of Parker, Pockett and Pitman, still live in Prestbury, the Parkers claiming descent from those who were Park Keepers for the Bishop of Hereford.

There are houses of stone, brick and timber, Cotswold stone roofs and thatch and in the background the green and pleasant slopes of Cleeve Hill. Prestbury is no ordinary village. Take time to discover the tranquillity of the ancient churchyard, the rural charm of winding lanes, and the historic centre. Perhaps then you will understand why many say "this is a place I am glad to have known."

Refreshments

The Plough, Mill Street: Traditional thatched country Inn. Bar snacks; Garden.

The Royal Oak, The Burgage: Also traditional country Inn. Bar food. Formerly owned by Tom Graveney.

The Kings Arms, High Street: 17th century Beefeater Inn, where Fred Archer "ate his first porridge". Bar snacks, lunches and suppers.

Prestbury House Hotel, The Burgage: Three star hotel; Accommodation; Leisure breaks; Activity weekends; Good food. Tel: 0242 529533

Nearby Attractions

Museum of Fashion, Pump Rooms: Open end of May to September. Tuesdays to Saturdays, Sunday and Bank Holidays.

Steeplechasing, Prestbury Park: In season. National Hunt Festival March.

2

WINCHCOMBE AND SUDELEY CASTLE

Winchcombe is a place to stir thoughts of the past for Kings, Queens, Abbots and Bishops have passed this way. King Kenulf lived in the walled Saxon city and when the body of his murdered son Kenelm was brought here pilgrims flocked to his shrine. Their gifts were a source of wealth to the Abbey, which not only became rich but also famed for its learning, the last Abbot being Richard Kydderminster, friend of Wolsey, a scholar and historian.

Alas, the Abbey was destroyed, like so many others, by the order of Henry VIII. After its destruction the town declined but the people have always remained independent of mind, prepared to stand up for their rights.

After tobacco was introduced in England it was grown successfully in Winchcombe, but when this was forbidden, Winchcombe folk were slow to obey orders. Cromwell's mounted troops came in 1658 to enforce the law, but the townspeople fought so hard the soldiers were forced to withdraw. There are still some old timers prepared to proudly tell you that the first crops were planted in Winchcombe by Sir Walter Raleigh who introduced tobacco to England.

With so long a past, ghosts are to be expected in the town, but the townsfolk are surprisingly diffident about talking of them. Several people admitted to seeing a monk, however, who is said to walk along the aptly named COWL LANE. After his appearance was reported in the 1993 spring edition of the Winchcombe Pathfinder, a reader wrote to say that he thought he had seen him some years ago at about 11.45 p.m. one night:

"I was walking in the direction of the Library just past the side entrance to the Abbey and noticed a figure walking in front of me, wearing a long robe and flat type of hat. Momentarily I glanced down to the ground and when I looked up it had disappeared. I then realised it was a ghost I had been following."

Stocks in Winchcombe

According to the March 1993 edition of *The Pathfinder* there have been numerous sightings of monks, not only in COWL LANE, but also on the TERRACE close to the site of the Abbey, and reports sometimes describe one whose legs cannot be seen, so that he appears to be floating. This is not an unusual phenomena, however, as old paths were lower than the present ground levels.

Monks have been seen too on roads just outside Winchcombe, including a smiling one near to Postlip Hall, where a chapel was built in 1144 as a safe haven for travellers when robbery on the roads was rife.

When I visited the CORNER CUPBOARD INN, however, I found stories of more modern ghosts. Built about 1550 the Inn was formerly a farmhouse, built with stones from the Abbey ruins. Ron Cousins and his wife Sue were the landlords for about 14 years, and although they retired some 15 years ago they still live in Winchcombe, right opposite the Corner Cupboard.

They told me of the evening they heard footsteps upstairs:

"There was only one customer in the Bar at the time," Ron said, "and he was a very solid, unimaginative sort of person, but we all heard the steps. They ran diagonally across the room upstairs, pitter-patter, like those of a child. What startled us though was that they ran above us from one end of the building to the other – and you can't do that because there is a wall part way across. We went upstairs to look, but couldn't see anything unusual. We all heard them though; there was no mistake about that."

Ron had been told the ghost of a young girl haunted the rooms, but never saw her. Two friends, however, Miss Rowebridge and Miss Perry, who owned an Antique shop opposite the Corner Cupboard, told him they once saw the figure of a young girl wearing a long gown, which could have been a period dress, or it could have been a nightdress.

When Ron Cousins took over the Corner Cupboard his wife owned a collection of Victorian dolls, which she decided to sell. Having looked over them carefully she laid them out neatly on her bed, and then went downstairs to meet the person who wanted to buy them. She was only out of the room for a few minutes, but when she returned the dolls had been thrown in a jumble all over the bed.

While the Cousins were running the Inn one of their staff, named Gwen, liked to sit at a table in the Bar in the evenings with a glass of cider in front of her, but from time to time it seemed to be deliberately emptied into her lap.

According to her daughter, "It always happened when she wore a particular blue dress".

After she died some of the customers claimed to have seen her in the middle of the room, and also at the foot the stairs.

The present owner, Sue Nash, would dearly like to know more about the young girl, whose footsteps she also hears. On the other hand she keeps a level head and does not let her imagination run away with her, as can sometimes happen to visitors.

Sue is a cat lover and has two at present, but her favourite, Presley, died a short time ago at the age of 17. In his last years a litter tray was put in the kitchen for him. "He was very good and always used it," Sue explained, "But he behaved as if he intended to dig down to Australia!"

Adjoining the kitchen is the Malthouse, now converted into holiday flats, where a Visitors' Book is kept, and Sue was a little taken aback to find a holiday-maker's complimentary comments ended with the words, "It was all perfect, and only enhanced by the ghostly scratchings in the night."

Vineyard Street, Winchcombe

The lovely church in Winchcombe is well worth a visit, and it is salutary to remember that the famous Henry Ford, of car fame, once cast covetous eyes on it! In 1929, he was building and equipping Greenfield village and museum in U.S.A. and looking for buildings in England which he could buy, dismantle, ship overseas then reassemble. Fortunately he was not allowed to have the church; instead, he bought Rose Cottage (for £500) in the village of Chedworth not many miles away.

With a name like Murder Alley it seemed reasonable to expect to find a ghost, but although I was told it was the site of the murder by a local butcher of his bride, because he thought she has been flirting at the wedding reception, all that has been left behind I was told is "an eerie, unpleasant feeling".

I was not disappointed, however, when I arranged a visit to nearby SUDELEY CASTLE for members of staff were willing and eager to tell of what they had seen or heard.

Scenes of grandeur and of tragedy have been enacted at SUDELEY, some in the banqueting hall which dates from 1470, but is now in ruins. Elizabeth I visited the castle three times, and while Catherine of Aragon, first wife of Henry VIII was there she spent time embroidering the Altar cloth still to be seen in the church at Winchcombe. One of the most notable occupants of the castle, however, was perhaps Catherine Parr, sixth and last wife of Henry VIII. After his death in 1547 she married Thomas Seymour, who brought her from Snowshill Manor to live at Sudeley, although her time there was short as she died in childbirth a year later.

I was told that the room in which she died is never warm, and the nursery, prepared for the child, in the oldest part of the castle, is always freezing cold. Around the anniversary of Catherine's death there is always a feeling of uneasiness in the castle, and sometimes a worried looking maid has been seen running from the nursery.

A few years ago, a tourist took photographs in the ruined part of the castle, and later sent one to the castle office because it showed a knight on horseback, bending to bid farewell to a lady clad in medieval dress.

Ghosts from other centuries are seen at Sudeley too. A woman in Victorian style clothes is seen in the grounds at times, but vanishes into thin air if challenged. Another in crinoline and bonnet kneels in prayer in the CHAPEL, and a man in a quaint velvet suit is also seen there.

There is a modern ghost too, believed to be that of Janet, the housekeeper who died after years of service in the castle. A very tidy person she was a strict disciplinarian. Her steps still retain a label, "Janet's steps. DO NOT USE," and a member of staff who sometimes uses them confessed, "I always felt a bit guilty when I do. I don't know whether there's any connection or not, but I lose my dusters then; no matter where I put them, they always disappear".

Since Janet's death her apartments have been converted into a public dining room. A male employee who knew her told of strange and unaccountable happenings. "I always like to put my tools away tidily," he said, "But of course when I'm working they get scattered about a bit. One day I was called away in the middle of a job, but when I got back my tools were lying in apple-pie order. I was puzzled but now I know if I go to tea and leave them about, they'll be in place when I get back".

Another time he was working in the dining room, which is long and rather narrow, when he saw a light passing right down the room. "It looked like a candle being carried," he said, "I couldn't see anything but the light and I watched it pass right down the whole length of the room and through the door at the far end".

Perhaps the most eerie happening was one which occurred on a day when the dining room was full of visitors and the waitresses were exceptionally busy. One of them carried a heavily laden tray towards the kitchens, but as she reached the door at the end of the room, two hands appeared in front of her and pushed it open! In her fright she dropped the tray, smashing most of the china on it.

Some employees at the castle live on the estate with their families. Mrs. Spencer Jones, who was living at NORTH LODGE told me of a happy ghost, that of a child.

"When my husband obtained a job at SUDELEY CASTLE some years ago," she said, "We moved from the north of England to live in one of the lodges, an attractive stone house about 100 years old.

Not long after we arrived I began to hear the sound of a child's laughter, the scuffling of shoes, and the yapping of a playful dog. I was puzzled, but not alarmed, and didn't say anything to my husband at first; then one day I asked if he'd heard anything unusual". "Yes," he said, "It sounds as if a child and a dog are playing and chasing a ball".

Some weeks later, my husband was talking to an old man who had lived in Winchcombe, not far from the lodge, for the whole of his life, who suddenly asked, "Do you ever hear that child?"

"What child?," my husband said.

"Well, many years ago a couple lived at that lodge with their little girl. The lodge was pretty isolated in those days, and the child had no playmates, but she had a dog and the two were inseparable. Then the little girl became ill. She was ill for a long time and eventually died. The dog just seemed to pine away after that, but people who've lived there since say they hear a child and a dog playing together."

"When we'd been living at the lodge for a few months my mother came down from the north to stay with us. She's stone deaf so I didn't tell her about the sounds we heard, but it was a funny thing, when she'd been here a few days she came smiling into the kitchen and said to me, 'I suppose you must be very friendly with your neighbours as you let that child and her dog come into the house to play'. She eventually saw the child. We never have, but sometimes when I hear a dog scratching at the door I go and open it, forgetting there won't be one there".

The Walk

Route: Back Lane car park – Cowl Lane – High Street – Gloucester Street – Cheltenham Road – Corndean Lane – Vineyard Street – Sudeley Park – Rushley Lane – Silk Mill Lane – Hailes Street – Chandos Street – North Street – Back Lane.

Distance: $3^1/_4$ miles.

Terrain: Town pavements, field paths (and minor roads). Gentle gradients only.

Finding Winchcombe: Winchcombe lies on the B4632 (formerly A46) between Cheltenham and Broadway. O.S. Landranger Sheet 163 (Cheltenham and Cirencester).

Park and Start: Free car park behind library in Back Lane Winchcombe. GR 023285.

The Route

❑ From the library car park follow the 'Town Centre' sign along COWL LANE.

❑ At its end, turn right along High Street. The site of Winchcombe Abbey is over the high wall on the right.

❑ Beyond Abbey Terrace on the left is Vineyard Street (formerly Duck Street) leading to SUDELEY CASTLE.

❑ Next comes the Parish Church, dedicated to St. Peter. Opposite stands the Jacobean House, dating from 1618 and formerly a grammar school. Behind can be glimpsed the Chandos Almshouses, built to house twelve poor women by Dorothy, Lady Chandos, in 1573.

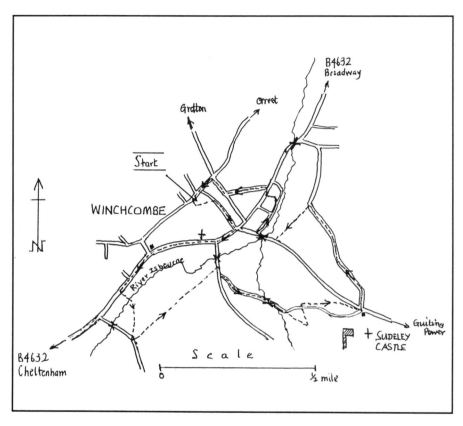

At the junction of Gloucester Street and Malthouse Lane stands the CORNER CUPBOARD INN. Built as a farmhouse in the 16th century, it has a bust of Benjamin Disraeli over the entrance.

Almost opposite is Rabbit Box House, on which can be seen carved stones, including one of a rabbit, taken from the destroyed Abbey.

Beyond Tobacco Close, cross the B4632 to follow a public footpath sign down to a footbridge over the river Isbourne.

Climb a sloping field and then veer right to reach Corndean Lane over a stile by a lamp standard.

❑ Leave the lane immediately over another stile alongside and follow the clear footpath over two more stiles and across a field to reach Vineyard Street through a kissing gate close to a bridge.

❑ Turn right and pass Almsbury Farm. At a fork, keep left along the drive to SUDELEY CASTLE. Cross a bridge and continue as far as a gate on the right. Enter SUDELEY PARK here, following a track with a fence on the left, round to a kissing gate.

❑ Follow the yellow arrows, keeping a fence on the left. SUDELEY CASTLE can be seen on the right. Cross the drive over two stiles and veer right to go over another in a fence. Continue across the park, following the waymarks, to leave over a stile by the main exit.

❑ Turn right along the road. In 50 yards, on the right, is NORTH LODGE.

❑ The route continues along Rushley Lane opposite. Follow this for almost half a mile, leaving it through a kissing gate on the left immediately after a drive at a right-hand bend.

❑ Follow the footpath sign over old ridge and furrow to a kissing gate by a cottage, leading to a narrow alley. At the foot, turn right along Castle Street.

❑ After crossing a bridge, turn right into Silk Mill Lane. Follow this for 300 yards, as far as a lamp standard and a block of garages. Turn left here up MURDER ALLEY. This leads to Hailes Street.

❑ Turn right, then left along Chandos Street, to reach North Street,

❑ Turn right here, then left at a crossroads along Back Lane to return to the car park.

Points of Interest

Winchcombe has been a town for over 1000 years and even had its own county for a short period in pre-Conquest times. Before then, as the chief city of the kingdom of Mercia, it was chosen as the site for a Benedictine Abbey, founded in 798 A.D. by King Kenulf.

It was the mysterious death of Kenulf's son, Kenelm, that led to Winchcombe becoming a popular place of pilgrimage. In 821 A.D. at his father's death, the boy king is said to have been murdered by his tutor,

Ashobert, on instructions from his jealous sister, Quendrida while out on a hunting expedition in the Clent Hills. According to legend, the decapitated body of the boy king was brought to Winchcombe Abbey for burial alongside his father, the story being substantiated to some extent by the discovery of two stone coffins, one large, one small, in the abbey grounds some years ago.

Winchcombe Abbey was utterly destroyed after the Dissolution of the Monasteries by Henry VIII and its stone used for building purposes for miles around.

St. Peter's church, built in the 1470s, has a wonderful collection of gargoyles, some of which are said to represent notables of the time, including the Abbot of the adjacent abbey and Ralph Boteler, builder of Sudeley Castle. As one of Gloucestershire's finest 'wool' churches the interior of St. Peter's has much beautiful work and is well worth seeing.

The street name 'Tobacco Close', passed on the walk, indicates that the town was once a centre for tobacco cultivation. Several fields in and around the town were planted with the crop and despite the attempts of the government to ban it in the interests of the Virginia trade, illicit tobacco-growing continued until the end of the 17th century.

Two interesting features lying just off the route of the walk are worth seeing. At the junction of High Street and North Street is the former pilgrim's inn, later the George Hotel, recently converted into apartments. This inn, built in 1490, was equipped with a pilgrim's gallery, the surviving section of which can be seen from the doorway, which itself bears the initials of an eminent abbot, Richard Kydderminster.

Across the road, outside the Town Hall and Tourist Information Centre, are Winchcombe's seven-hole stocks, said to have been made to accommodate a one-legged 'regular'!

Like Winchcombe, nearby Sudeley Castle has a long and colourful history. Although a castle was first built on the site in Norman times, it was during the mid 15th century that Admiral Ralph Boteler built the present structure. Henry VIII is said to have brought Anne Boleyn here and his widow Katherine Parr spent her last years as lady of the manor on her marriage to Sir Thomas Seymour, Baron Sudeley.

After being 'slighted' following the Civil War, Sudeley Castle fell on hard times. It took the dedication of its 19th century owners, the Dents, glove-makers of Worcester, to restore the building to something resembling its past glory.

Today Sudeley is a highly popular tourist attraction, with castle, gardens and spacious parkland, providing a great deal to interest the visitor.

Refreshments

The Corner Cupboard, Gloucester Street, Winchcombe: Traditional Inn; Bar meals; Garden; Malthouse holiday accommodation. Tel: 0242 602303

The Plaisterers' Arms, The Crescent: Traditional Inn. Bar meals.

The White Hart Hotel, High Street: Historic hotel. Bar meals.

The White Lion Hotel, North Street: Historic hotel. Bar meals.

Sudeley Castle, Winchcombe: Restaurant; Gardens; Gift Shop and Holiday Cottages. Castle open 1st April/31st October – 11 am to 5 pm. Gardens – 10.30 am/5.30 pm. Tel: 0242 602308.

Several good restaurants, cafes and other pubs nearby in Winchcombe.

Nearby Attractions

Winchcombe Railway Museum, Gloucester Street, Winchcombe: Easter/October, Admission charge.

Winchcombe Folk Museum: March/October.

Toddington Railway Centre, Toddington, Nr. Winchombe: Opening times vary. Tel: 0242 602462.

3

KINETON COUNTRY

The ancient inns and hotels to be found throughout the length and breadth of Britain have housed men and women of all classes over the centuries. Weary travellers have stepped from stage coaches or alighted from horses to thankfully accept warmth and hospitality at isolated inns, for as Dr. Johnson said, "There is nothing which has been contrived by man, by which so much happiness is produced as by a good tavern or inn".

Kineton

Not every traveller was involved in legitimate business, and card sharpers waited at some inns for the unwary. Tradition has it too that horsemen fleeing from justice turned their horses' shoes around so that their tracks seemed to lead in the opposite direction, but those galloping through the Cotswolds had a much better trick; their horses were shod with circular shoes!

Landlords were sometimes in league with them too, ready to provide a hiding place for rider and horse, and to supply food as well as shelter. Even today there is a certain sympathy for the highwaymen of old and an air of romance surrounds their legendary exploits. Dick Turpin's name is not only known and his exploits remembered today, although it was as long ago as 1739 that he was finally caught and hanged at the Mount, outside the walls of York, but his grave in the town is still visited regularly.

Perhaps it is because of the danger, excitement and fear which surrounded those wild races through the night that has left restless ghosts in many an isolated inn, like that one who it is said burst through the door of the HALFWAY HOUSE at Kineton . . .

Having heard several versions of the story I visited the Halfway House to investigate, but the landlady asked me not to question her husband.

"He's scared about it," she said, "So he gets angry if anyone asks questions".

She gave me the name instead of an elderly man, Fred Meadows, who claimed to have seen the ghost, so I visited him at the old people's home at Bourton on the Water where he was living, and this is his story:

"I was born and brought up in Kineton, a few miles from here, and lived there until two years ago when I moved into this old people's home.

Kineton, as you know, is still only a tiny hamlet, even though a few big modern houses were built a few years ago, but when I was young it was very isolated and we saw few strangers. The village had scarcely changed for hundreds of years, except that there used to be a forge opposite the old pub, The Halfway House. Everyone in the village knows everyone else, so although it was a very quiet isolated place when I was young we made our own enjoyment. There were no lights in the lanes, of course, and it was pitch dark in the winter, but the Halfway House was always a warm and friendly place so although we didn't have much money to spend, we would be pretty sure of meeting friends there on a winter night.

When I was about eighteen (and I'm seventy-eight now), I walked up there one very black night just before Christmas to join my friends. I suppose there were about twenty of us there, when suddenly we heard the sound of a horse galloping madly up the dark road.

Somebody asked, "What's that?," and then there was a terrible sound like wind roaring and moaning and shrieking, shaking the door and whistling through the keyhole. Everybody jumped up as the door burst open, and there was a wild looking man glaring at us. He was wearing a black coat, or cape and a high hat; not a top hat but more like a woman's hat. He was no ordinary man and the sound of the wind was terrible. I've never been so frightened in all my life, not before nor since.

Everybody ran! I went through the back door. I think some got out through the front, I don't know how, but you've never seen a pub empty so quick. I'll never forget it as long as I live.

There's always been a legend in Kineton that one winter night, long ago, a highwayman galloped into the village. He was flying for his life, but his horse had lost a shoe so he hammered on the door of the blacksmith's cottage and made the man get up from his bed to shoe the horse. Then he ran across to the HALFWAY HOUSE, banged on the door, and forced the landlord to give him food and drink.

Whether he was caught that night or not I don't know, but I reckon it was his ghost who burst into the pub and terrified us. I wouldn't like to see him again."

Whether he has been seen again since I do not know, nor why he appeared on that occasion, unless it was the anniversary of the night the highwayman rode for his life, but although Fred Meadows saw him more than half a century ago he shivered as he told me the story, and repeated "I wouldn't like to see him again."

Perhaps he never will come again. Although the village is still small many visitors arrive at the inn by car or on foot during the summer. But I am not sure what it is like there in the winter when the nights are long and dark!

The Walk

Route: Car park – Castlett Farm – Kineton – Castlett Wood – car park.

Distance: 3³/₄ miles.

Terrain: Minor roads, tracks and field paths. A few gentle climbs.

Finding Kineton: Kineton lies between the B4077 and the B4068, 1¹/₂ miles north of Guiting Power. O.S. Landranger Sheet 163 (Cheltenham and Cirencester).

Park and Start: Small free car park, 1¹/₂ miles SW of Kineton. Best reached from Winchcombe – Guiting Power road along single-track gated road signposted Kineton, from crossroads 1 mile NW of Guiting Power. Corral-like car park is on right, three-quarters of a mile along road. GR 085259.

The Route

❑ From the car park approach, walk to the crossroads and turn left down the roughly-surfaced track. Follow this for about half a mile to a T-junction.

❑ Turn left (Warden's Way sign). Opposite silos, descend a stony path between hedges. At the foot of the slope, turn left to cross a tiny bridge.

❑ Climb a bank, go through a handgate, and continue along a field path to reach Castlett Farm. Follow the drive and after passing between gateposts, cross a lane and follow a footpath sign through a gateway opposite.

❑ Climb steps and cross two stiles. Keep a hedge on the right up to a gate.

❑ Keep the same line to cross a stile. Immediately beyond, go through a gap and keep a hedge on the right to reach Kineton through a farm gateway.

❑ Turn left along the road. The Halfway House is straight on. The route turns right in 30 yards, down a lane. At its foot, cross the River Windrush and turn left.

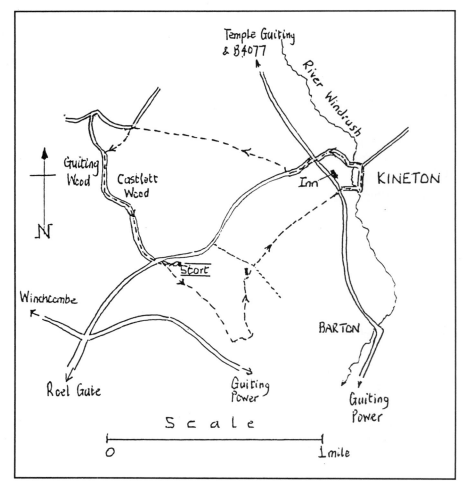

☐ Continue along a lane, keeping left at a junction to reach and cross the river once more.

☐ Climb the lane back to Kineton. The inn is now on the left. To continue the walk, turn right and then left at the Roel Gate signpost.

☐ In 250 yards, turn right up a lane (unsuitable for motors). Follow this for almost a mile, until it dips to join a surfaced road coming in from the right.

❑ Turn left here along a grassy track. (Notice the toad carved from limestone block).

❑ The track soon narrows and passes an old mill leat before reaching a road.

❑ Turn left along this road, passing through a gate by a cottage to reach the crossroads and the car park.

The toad carving

Points of Interest

Not to be confused with the Warwickshire town of the same name, Kineton is a hamlet midway between Temple Guiting and Guiting Power. Scattered amongst the newer houses are several traditional Cotswold farms and cottages, some of which date from the 17th century.

Kineton stands on the west bank of the River Windrush, which rises near Taddington, a few miles to the north. The route provides the chance to walk alongside this youthful river, a tributary of the Thames. Two footbridges are crossed alongside fords, the first of which is an enchanting little structure with its stonework encrusted with liverworts.

The last stretch of the walk is routed along a delightful wooded valley, that of a tributary stream of the Windrush. Though small, this stream once powered a water mill, the remains of which can be seen on the edge of Castlett Wood. During spring and summer this walk is especially rich in lime-loving wild flowers and the bird life, both in the wooded stretches and by the waterside, provides further interest throughout.

Refreshments

Halfway House, Kineton: Traditional country Inn. Bar snacks; Garden.

Approx. 1 mile: Farmers' Arms, Guiting Power: Traditional country Inn. Bar snacks.

The New Inn, Guiting Power: Traditional country Inn. Bar snacks.

Nearby Attractions

Cotswold Farm Park and Rare Breeds Survival Centre, Benborough, Nr. Guiting Power: Open Easter/end of September. Admission charge. Tel: 04517 850307.

4

HAILES ABBEY, DIDBROOK AND STANWAY

Stanway village is regarded by many as one of the gems of the Cotswolds, a haven of peace and beauty, whilst STANWAY HOUSE, with its Jacobean gateway, is indescribably romantic.

It is the home of Lord Neidpath, a philanthropic landlord determined to preserve the character of the village, who has resisted all temptations to sell houses to outsiders; consequently, this is no week-end dormitory village but the home of families who have lived in Stanway for generations.

Many famous people have stayed in Stanway House, including writers and artists. Lady Cynthia Asquith lived here during World War I and it was here that she worked as a secretary to J.M. Barrie when he wrote Peter Pan. He lived at Stanway House for some time, and was responsible for the building of the thatched cricket pavilion, standing on staddle stones, to be seen from the lane nearby.

The House is well worth a visit but if you are unlucky enough to arrive on a day when it is closed, enter the churchyard and walk right around the outside of the church until you stand facing the magnificent bay window, with its 1056 latticed panes. Lady Cynthia Asquith wrote of it in her diary, "so mellowed by time that whenever the sun shines through their amber and green glass, the effect is a vast honeycomb".

Before you enter the church look for the stone coffin and Saxon cross set into the wall of the churchyard, as well as the 14th century tithe barn built for the Abbot of Tewkesbury.

The OLD VICARAGE which stands in the lane opposite the church porch has been converted into three cottages, and when I visited Mrs. Norton, in the end one nearest to Stanway House I heard of many strange happenings.

Stanway cricket pavillion

About 10 years ago, around 1 p.m. there would often be a smell of tobacco smoke and then the sitting room door would quietly open. This became so common an occurrence that once, when it opened just as her daughter reached it, she absent-mindedly said "Thank you"!

When the Nortons first moved into the house they found a collection of fossils on the window sill. They were not particularly attractive and Mrs. Norton decided to remove them, but as she picked them up she was startled to see the clock fly off the wall. Deciding discretion was the better part of valour she replaced them. "I don't really like them," she told me, "But I think they are best left alone".

A ship's bell hangs over the mantle-piece. One day when her sister and brother-in-law were visiting they sat in front of the fire with Mr. and Mrs Norton. "Suddenly," she said, "The bell was rung imperiously, as if someone was ringing for service".

There is a pretty garden outside the cottage where a path had been made at some time with old gravestones. When Mr. Norton moved them to re-plan the garden there were several disturbances until the work was finished.

One day there was a frightening incident while Mr. Norton was working in the churchyard. His lawn mower started to run rapidly backwards towards a coffin bier, and he was completely unable to stop it. Just before a crash seemed inevitable it stopped abruptly of its own accord, as if by unseen hands, and Mr. Norton heard himself gasp "Thank you!"

The Nortons only guess at the identity of their ghost, whose footsteps they hear pacing up and down in the attic, but they are accustomed to him now and are not afraid.

On occasions too they hear a horse gallop past the cottage in the middle of the night which cannot be seen, but although he travels fast Mrs. Norton has the impression he is lame.

A former maid at STANWAY HOUSE told me there is no tradition of hauntings but when she worked there one of the windows would open and close as if by unseen hands. On several occasions too she, and the husband of another member of staff, saw an elderly man, wearing a stove pipe hat, sitting by the fire in the Great Hall, although no one knew who he was.

Ghostly horses are not uncommon in the Cotswolds as has already been demonstrated, nor are phantom monks, but in spite of the proximity of HAILES ABBEY there is no tradition of monks haunting the village.

I was given a strange story concerning BECKBURY CAMP by a lady who lives lower down the hill. She has a large Alsatian dog which has never been afraid of anything, so she has happily walked in lonely places with him feeling completely safe. Until, that is, on the evening when she was walking with him as dusk was falling. Encountering a muddy patch she left the usual path intending to pass close to the Camp site.

Suddenly, to her complete astonishment, the dog stopped dead, hair on end, and refused to move. She tried to persuade him, then ordered him to walk, without avail. He would not budge and when she tried to drag him with her he wrenched the lead out of her hand and raced for home, where she found him panting and evidently still in a state of fear.

What did he see, I wonder? Unfortunately, we shall never know.

High up on the hills, not far from the Camp, stands HAYLES FARM, commanding magnificent views across the countryside. The farmer and his wife, Mr. and Mrs. Harrell, live in a modern house a few yards downhill from the Farm Shop, where doors open at times, without the knobs turning, and then are quietly closed. "We can't have a ghost," Mrs. Harrell told me, "Because the house isn't old".

When I assured her I had many stories of modern houses being haunted she replied, "Well then perhaps it's a monk. After all we're very near Hailes Abbey".

Beyond the Farm Shop over the crest of the hill is a reservoir. One day a Gipsy working near there came running to her, looking very scared, saying he had seen the figure of a woman in a crinoline near the reservoir. Who she was, or why she was there no one could say, but the farm is old and many types of people have worked there over the years.

Once, looking down from the farm, thousands of sheep would have been seen in the valley belonging to the monks of HAILES ABBEY for like many in the Cotswolds they too derived income from sheep.

Hailes Abbey was one of the last Cistercian Houses to be founded in England. Richard, Earl of Cornwall and King of the Romans, founded the Abbey after making a vow to do so when he was in danger at sea in October 1242. When it was dedicated on 5th November 1251 there was a remarkable ceremony attended by the King, Queen Eleanor, Earl Richard and "a very large company of nobles and 13 Bishops" although at that time Gloucestershire must have been an extremely remote place and the Abbey became the mecca for a vast number of pilgrims.

It is in ruins now but it is still possible to visualise the beauty it must once have had and the nearby museum contains many treasures and interesting relics.

There is a great sense of peace and no tradition of hauntings, but monasteries were not always happy places. Punishments were severe and violent death not unknown, and a person I met who lives nearby told me, "I love this place but I always felt it was a place of evil as well as great good, although I had no reason to know that. One day though I was walking down the lane, near to the entrance, when I was suddenly overwhelmed by a feeling of great fear. My hair rose on the back of my neck and I stopped in my tracks. It was all over in a few minutes, and I've never experienced it again, but I shall never forget it".

Ley lines are said to crisscross the site, as they do at many historic and haunted places. Maybe one day we shall learn more about them and whether they have any influence here.

Hailes Church stands almost opposite the Abbey and you will be well rewarded if you spare time to enter. Built 100 years before the Abbey it contains wonderful wall paintings.

Opposite the doors is a huge figure of St. Christopher, treading through dangerous waters, staff in hand and, just to be discerned, the Christ child on his shoulders.

In the splays of the half blocked Norman windows in the east wall of the chancel you will find full length paintings of St. Catherine of Alexandria and St. Margaret of Antioch, and a fascinating collection of figures from the bestiary adorn several other walls.

The Walk

Route: Hailes Abbey – Didbrook – Stanway – Wood Stanway – Beckbury Camp – Hailes Abbey.

Distance: $4^3/_4$ miles.

Terrain: Chiefly along fairly level footpaths, though with a longish climb from Wood Stanway to Beckbury Camp.

Finding Hailes Abbey: Hailes Abbey lies half a mile east of the B4632, three miles NE of Winchcombe. O.S. Landranger Sheet 150 (Worcester and the Malverns).

Park and Start: Abbey car park (National Trust). GR 051301.

The Route

❏ From the ABBEY car park, walk back towards the B4632, passing the church on the right. Bear right at a T-junction and on reaching a left-hand bend, turn right along a track, signposted as a public footpath to STANWAY.

❏ After crossing a stile, ignore the yellow waymark pointing to the right. Instead, keep straight on to pass through a field gate on the left. Follow a fence on the right to reach a road through a second gate.

❏ Turn right into Didbrook. Keep right at a fork to pass the church and school, both on the left. Beyond a double bend, turn left to follow a public footpath sign along the edge of a wood.

❏ Cross four stiles to reach the B4077.

❏ Turn right along the verge and continue for 250 yards, then cross to go over a stile and down a slope. Cross a stream and a stile and pass between a fence and a wall to reach a lane leading to a road at Stanway. (The church, HOUSE and obelisk can be seen straight ahead).

❏ For view of the HOUSE, tithe barn and cricket pavilion standing on staddle stones, turn left.

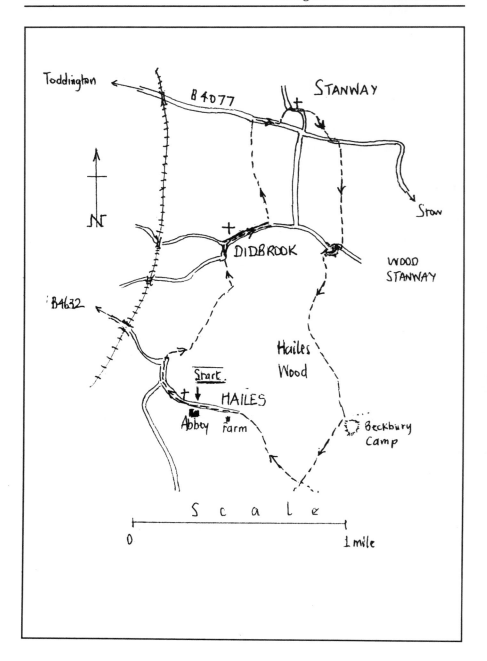

Toddington

B 4077

STANWAY

N

Stow

B4632

DIDBROOK

WOOD
STANWAY

Hailes
Wood

Spark.

HAILES

Abbey Farm

Beckbury
Camp

S c a l e

0   1 mile

❑ Continue the route by turning right. Pass the church on the left, opposite which is the OLD VICARAGE. Beyond the gate-house and the wall, follow the Cotswold Way sign to the left. Go through a kissing-gate (noting the swan's head carving) and pass through an old orchard to reach the B4077 once more over a stile.

❑ Turn left along the pavement for 50 yards before crossing to follow the Cotswold Way to Wood Stanway, reached via three stiles and two gates. On reaching a road, turn right, then left at a fork. The road swings to the right to end at a field gate.

❑ Go through and follow the left-hand waymark up the field side to pass through a gate. Keep woodland on the right, climbing steadily, with extensive views opening up behind. When the route levels out somewhat follow the waymark over a low fence and continue climbing, crossing two stiles in fences.

❑ Beyond the second of these, at the limit of the wood, follow the fence on the left up the slope to meet the Cotswold Way once more, just below BECKBURY CAMP.

❑ After seeing the Camp, and the monument, follow the Cotswold Way across sheep pasture, passing through two gates to reach a stile leading to the stony pilgrims' path climbing from HAILES ABBEY up to Farmcote.

❑ Turn right down this path, passing HAILES FARM on the left, back to Hailes Abbey and the car park.

Points of Interest

A romantic ruin, two attractive Cotswold villages, a remote hamlet, a mysterious monument and a prehistoric camp – all these feature on this delightful scenic walk along and around the northern stretch of the Cotswold Way long-distance footpath.

The Cistercian Abbey of Hailes, the starting place, was for centuries one of the greatest centres for pilgrimage in England. It was founded by the crusading Richard, Earl of Cornwall, the younger brother of Henry III, in 1245, in thanksgiving for having survived shipwreck, and both the King and Queen were present at its dedication several years later.

Hailes gained its reputation among pilgrims in 1270 when Edmund, Richard's son, presented the abbot with a phial said to contain Christ's blood.

Almost 300 years later, in 1538, this relic was revealed as a fake – a mixture of honey and saffron – and in keeping with all the other monastic buildings, Hailes was destroyed on the order of Henry VIII and its treasures looted or otherwise dispersed. Today, Hailes Abbey, under the caring custody of the National Trust, is a beautiful though scanty ruin. With the help of its museum, however, visitors can obtain some impression of its former glory and in so doing appreciate why in his 'Canterbury Tales', Geoffrey Chaucer had the Pardoner swear 'by the blode of Crist that is in Hayles'.

Across from the Abbey lies Hailes church, a century older than its illustrious neighbour and itself well worth seeing on account of its 14th century wall paintings.

Didbrook is a pleasant little place with a 14th century church and a number of timber-framed cottages, some of which could well be Tudor in origin.

Stanway, by contrast, reveals Cotswold stone fashioned in the very best tradition. Outstanding is the gate-house of Stanway House, the work of local masons, the Strongs of Barrington, and built in the Renaissance style in the 17th century. Behind can be seen Stanway House itself, erected by the Tracys and possessing strikingly beautiful windows. Within the private grounds of the House, but glimpsed from the road, is the vast 14th century tithe barn in which was stored the Abbot of Tewkesbury's share of the medieval harvest. This building has been carefully maintained and re-roofed with authentic Cotswold slates.

Finally, Stanway has one other building of distinction – a timber and thatch cricket pavilion dating from the 1930s and standing on staddle stones, the gift to the village of Sir James Barrie, author of Peter Pan.

From Wood Stanway, a hamlet of spacious farmhouses well away from the busy world, the route climbs to Beckbury Camp. This is a six acre Iron Age fort, sited in a commanding position overlooking the Vale of Evesham and as yet untouched by the archaeologist's spade. At Beckbury's north west corner in a clump of beech trees is a monument known locally as Cromwell's Seat, said to have been erected by Thomas Cromwell, chancellor to Henry VIII and from which he is said to have viewed the demolition of Hailes Abbey.

The last stage of the walk follows the Cotswold Way down past a fruit farm and back to Hailes Abbey along a stony pilgrims' path.

Refreshments

The Old Bakehouse, Stanway: Tea Room – Cream teas, Open Easter to end September – 3 pm to 6 pm but closed on Mondays and Wednesdays.

Hayles Farm, Hailes: Farm shop and modern cafe. Open all year, Summer – 10 am/6 pm, Winter – 10 am/5 pm. Tel: 0242 602123

Pheasant Inn, Toddington (1 mile): Modernised Inn. Bar meals.

Nearby Attractions

Hailes Abbey, National Trust, Ruins and Museum: April 1st/September 30th – 10 am/6 pm. Earlier closing October/March. Tel: 0242 602398.

Stanway House, Stanway: Beautiful manor house. Frequently open to the public during summer months. Tel: 0386 73469.

5

STANTON AND SNOWSHILL

The walk described in this chapter linking Stanton and Snowshill is one of the longest in the book, but whether you intend to follow the whole route or not, many will no doubt be tempted to first wander quietly around Stanton, one of the loveliest villages in the Cotswolds.

The Cotswold stone houses seem to glow with a special warmth here, and as the date stones show many are between 300 and 400 years old. The village owes much, however, to Sir Philip Stott, a Lancashire architect who bought the estate in 1906 and lovingly restored many of the buildings during the next three decades.

The village even had a swimming pool from 1910 until recent years, thanks to his generosity, as after hearing of the death by drowning of a child in another village he was determined that every child in Stanton should have the chance to learn to swim. Although he died in 1937, there are still old-timers who speak of him with affection.

Set back from the main street, not far from the village cross, the spire of St. Michael's and All Angels church can be seen, from where the bells can be heard "In summertime on Bredon". Deep grooves on bench ends inside the church bear witness to the time when dogs were tethered by shepherds during services. It is believed stone benches existed in the church when seating accommodation was limited, and were used only by the old and infirm. Thence came the expression "the weakest shall go to the wall".

If you follow your map to the centre of the village, before turning towards Stanway Road you will see the wall of The Court, former home of Sir Philip Stott. In this wall is the War Memorial, converted by Sir Norman Comper from the village pump.

Immediately afterwards you will pass the Manor in the block of stone buildings on your right. Dating from the 15th century, its massive stone walls are nearly a metre thick. Some modernisation has taken place inside but the charm and beauty of the house have not been spoiled, although it must differ greatly from the way it looked in 1543 when Henry VIII gave it to Catherine Parr as part of her wedding gift. There is still a room there known as The King's Room.

At the side of the manor is a narrow PASSAGE WAY or ALLEY, where two rather eccentric elderly sisters once lived.

Several people claim to have seen the ghost of one of them. No wonder, for who would want to leave so beautiful a place? The strongest ghost story given to me in STANTON, however, is that of one to be found at THE MOUNT, the old inn set high on the hill at the other end of the village where your walk ends. The present landlord, Colin Johns, lives there with his wife and son Paul. They have a ghost whom they have named Billy, after a landlord of 50 years ago.

The Inn was formerly a farmhouse, but then became an Off Licence when Billy Richards lived there. In true Cotswold style he was called Billy Conk because of his big nose, but he made customers obey the rules. They were not allowed to drink on the premises and had to be consumed over the boundary.

A dart board was hung on an elm tree and a brazier kept burning to keep the players warm, but on windy nights it was not unknown for darts to fly though the air and down the hill.

Billy was a friendly host and is friendly now, but his ghost is heard not seen. Colin's wife told me she was first aware of him when she felt someone touch her shoulder as she hung out washing on the line.

"He often does it," she said, "But somehow it's a friendly gesture and I don't mind".

The first time her son Paul became aware of Billy though he was alarmed. "I was just dropping off to sleep one night," he told me, "When the door opened, footsteps came to my bedside, then turned and went out again, and I heard the door close".

He was nervous about it at first, but has got used to it now, as it happens fairly frequently.

When a twenty-year old friend came to stay and was put up in that room he was not told about the ghost. "He's not the nervous type," Paul's father said. "It never occurred to us he'd be afraid if he did hear anything"

They were wrong. He had the same experience as Paul, and rushed from the room in great agitation, and spent the rest of the night sleeping on the floor. He has steadfastly refused ever to sleep in Paul's room again.

Snowshill, the next village on your map, clings to the side of the hill and is a delight to the eye, but it is not the place where you would expect to find new inventions, yet it was here, in 1842, that one of the first sewing machines was made by Charles ("Schemer") Keyte. It is said to have helped in the evolution of the modern machine, and some years ago was presented to the Science Museum in South Kensington.

Pictures of it look odd today, but it is no more strange than the mechanical oddities to be found in SNOWSHILL MANOR.

This beautiful house, now owned by the National Trust, was once the gift of Henry VIII to his sixth wife, Catherine Parr. After his death she married Thomas Seymour and moved a few miles away to Sudeley Castle, but it was half a century later that a scandal occurred which still disturbs the house.

About 1566 Snowshill Manor came into the hands of the Warren family, who held it for 70 years. In 1604 the owner, John Warren, was related to Ann Parsons, a 16 year old heiress, who in that year was staying with her guardian at Elmley Castle, Worcestershire.

On St. Valentine's Eve a party of young men, led by Anthony Palmer, abducted Ann from her guardian's home and galloped away with her through the lonely Cotswold countryside to Snowshill Manor. There, in an UPSTAIRS ROOM at midnight she was married to Anthony Palmer by the Rev. Richard Stone, vicar of Broadway. Whether Ann was a party to the plan is not really known, but certainly Anthony Palmer was regarded as a fortune hunter and documentary evidence suggests that the marriage was eventually annulled.

Even if a willing partner, the mad ride through the night would have been an alarming experience for Ann: if she was abducted against her will, she must have been in a state of terror. It is fear, or terror, which seems to have been imposed on the atmosphere of the Upper Room where the marriage took place, making many visitors hesitate to enter.

When this became apparent is not clear, as the house has changed hands a number of times. It was in a state of disrepair when it was bought just after the First World War by an eccentric young man named Charles Wade, who restored it and filled it with an amazing collection of articles still to be seen in the house. Evidently aware of the strange atmosphere in that Upper Room, now known as ANN'S ROOM, he sent a fragment of wood from it to a clairvoyant. Without explaining where it came from he asked for her comments. She replied:

"In the lofty house in an Upper Room, late at night, there is a girl in a green dress of the 17th century – she is greatly agitated – she paces anxiously up and down the room – she doesn't live here and will not stay the night".

In 1983 the wife of the administrator told me that although she had lived in the house for several years she had never felt aware of any ghostly presence. "I must say though," she added, "Frequently when I am showing groups of people over the house, one of them will stop on the threshold of ANN'S ROOM and say, 'I don't want to go any further'. It could be coincidence – except that it always occurs just there, and it does seem to happen rather often."

J.B. Priestley visited Snowshill in 1953 and met Charles Wade, the owner of SNOWSHILL MANOR at that time, by chance and afterwards visited the house on several occasions. He described Wade as "the last of a famous company, the eccentric English country gentry". The house he termed "a Gothic craziness" but he was glad Wade was there "in the green cap among the hills".

If your visit to the village coincides with an Open Day at the Manor you will find every kind of mechanical oddity on view and also be able to test you own psychic powers as you step over the threshold into Ann's Room.

There is another supernatural story told about a 19th century owner of Snowshill Manor, named Charles Marshall whose widow continued to live there and to farm the land after his death. She employed a labourer named Carter who worked at Hill Farm, a remote spot linked to the village by lonely tracks. One dark night, on his way back to Snowshill he was startled to find the ghost of Charles Marshall riding beside him on a black pony, but he was to afraid too speak. After it had happened several times, however, he went to see the Rector and told him. "Next time," advised the Rector, "Say What troubleth thou here, in the Name of the Lord?"

Carter did this and the ghost told him to meet him at midnight when he would give him a secret message for Mrs. Marshall. When Carter did so he was given a message, but although no one was ever told what it was it was believed that Mrs. Marshall was given the location of hidden money, because afterwards she was able to have new buildings put up to the north of the Manor.

An unhappy monk is said to haunt the lane which runs past the Manor, and some villagers avoid walking there at night. There are stories too of a strange figure seen by a former landlord of the Snowshill Arms. Doors were said to be opened by a hooded figure, upsetting the landlord's dog. Who he is, or why he haunts the building no one knows, but it is believed that the Inn once housed visiting clergy and lay people. Perhaps he was among them.

The Walk

Route: Stanton- Shenberrow Hill – Littleworth Wood – Great Brockhampton Farm – Snowshill – Shenberrow Hill – Stanton.

Distance: 5³/₄ miles.

Terrain: Chiefly footpaths and bridleways. Muddy patches after rain. A few fairly steep slopes.

Finding Stanton: Stanton lies half a mile east of the B4632, between Winchombe and Broadway. O.S. Landranger Sheet 150 (Worcester and the Malverns).

Park and Start: Village free car park. GR 068343.

The Route

❑ From the car park, walk towards the centre of the village. Turn right at the road junction and follow the STANWAY ROAD as far as a signpost indicating Shenberrow Hill and the Cotswold Way at the entrance to the drive to Chestnut Farm.

❑ Cross the stile on the right at the bend in the drive and follow the bridleway sign up to a gate. From here, a clear track climbs steadily, passing through six more gates to reach the buildings of Shenberrow Farm.

❑ Keep straight on, following the Broadway sign, along a stony track between the buildings to cross a cattle grid and reach a T-junction. Turn right along the Cotswold Way and follow it as far as a staggered junction of tracks beyond another cattle grid.

❑ Turn right here, leaving the Cotswold Way. In 200 yards, turn left to enter Littleworth Wood (National Trust), over a stile. Follow the clear path through the wood and leave over another stile to reach a lane. SNOWSHILL can be seen straight ahead.

❑ Turn left down to a stile on the right, just before the drive to Great Brockhampton Farm. The route now follows a footpath along a tiny valley

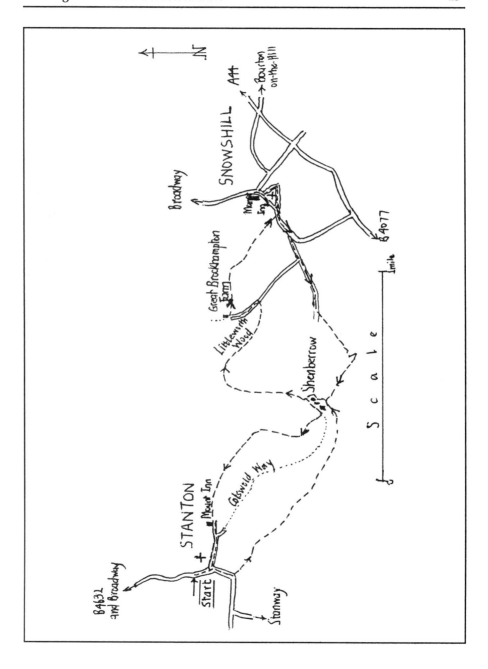

before crossing a stile and swinging right to follow a hedge on the left to another stile by a gate. Beyond, follow the yellow waymark round a field edge to join a track. Turn right along this to reach a gate and continue up to SNOWSHILL.

❑ At the top of the lane, turn left into the village. Keep left at the church. THE SNOWSHILL ARMS is on the left and beyond is the entrance to SNOWSHILL MANOR (National Trust).

❑ After exploring the village, return along the road walked earlier. Pass the end of the lane and continue to reach a second lane, also on the right, and shown as a no-through-road. Follow this, ignoring side turns, for one-third of a mile. Just beyond a right-hand bend, leave the road along what appears to be a track on the left to follow blue waymarks across two fields to reach a wide track.

❑ Turn left, and in 40 yards right, along another bridleway, which leads back to Shenberrow Farm. Retrace the outward route between the buildings as far as the T-junction.

❑ At this point, turn left along the Cotswold Way. Go through the gate to the right of the farmhouse.

❑ Two alternative descents back to STANTON are possible from here:

1. The more straightforward route, along the Cotswold Way, entails following the clear waymarks (yellow arrows and white dots) down to the village street, from which the MOUNT INN is reached by a short climb to the right.

2. To take a more varied route, leading directly to the Mount Inn, turn right and follow the line indicated by the yellow waymark by the wall. This entails descending over rough ground, crossing a track and entering woodland through a gate. Inside the wood, the path swings left and descends steeply to a stile.

❑ Beyond, turn right along a well-used path (muddy after rain) to reach a spring by a ruined barn. 50 yards beyond, follow the yellow waymark to the left along a path which eventually leaves the wood to reach an area of sloping ground.

❑ Instead of descending towards the covered reservoir below, cross the slope diagonally to pass through gaps in a double wooden fence. Keep the same line through two gates to join a track.

❑ Turn left to reach the MOUNT INN. The car park is on the right at the foot of the hill, beyond the church.

Snowshill

Points of Interest

Less than two miles apart as the crow flies, Stanton and Snowshill are linked by footpaths which by their wriggling add considerably to the distance, but compensate by giving plenty of variety to this longer-than-average walk.

Stanton, its one street climbing the Cotswold edge to peter out at the aptly-named Mount Inn, is deservedly regarded as one of the loveliest villages in the region. Not a stone seems out of place, with every farmhouse and cottage fitting perfectly into the timeless scene.

In keeping with the rest of the village is the parish church, standing back from the street, yet with its graceful spire, backed by noble beeches, adding further beauty. Norman in origin, it comprises chiefly Perpendicular work and contains among other treasures a Jacobean pulpit from which John Wesley preached and stained glass salvaged from Hailes Abbey.

Above Stanton, crowning the ridge at over 900 feet above sea level, is SHENBERROW HILL, with its farm set amid the ramparts of an Iron Age hill fort, which when excavated yielded a bronze bracelet and an iron knife.

Snowshill too, is an alluring village, perched, as its name suggests, high on the wolds, where it bears the brunt of severe winters. Its cottages are grouped engagingly around its unremarkable church and its two most sought-after buildings, the Snowshill Arms and the Manor, are near neighbours close-by. Snowshill Manor is a superb Tudor building with a south front dating from the William and Mary period. It stands in terraced gardens commanding sweeping views and is famous for its incredible display of bygones collected by Charles Paget Wade, who gave the house and its contents to the National Trust before emigrating to the West Indies.

Refreshments

Mount Inn, Stanton: Traditional Inn. Wonderful views from garden. Bar snacks.

The Manor, Stanton: Accommodation; Cream teas in garden on summer Sundays. Tel: 0386 73513

Snowshill Arms, Snowshill: Traditional Cotswold Inn. Bar snacks.

Nearby Attractions:

Snowshill Manor, National Trust, Snowshill: Open Saturday/Sunday. April/October. Easter Saturday, Sunday and Monday. Open May to end September. Wednesday to Sunday and Bank Holiday Mondays. Admission charge.

Broadway Tower Country Park: two miles north-east of Snowshill. April/October seven days per week. Admission charge.

6

TEWKESBURY

Tewkesbury has much to offer the discerning visitor. The largest town in the north of the County it has a magnificent Abbey, medieval houses, quaint alleys, historic inns, literary associations, modern shops and two wide rivers, the Warwickshire Avon and the Severn, as well as many ghosts.

There were monks in Tewkesbury hundreds of years before William the Conqueror arrived and a decisive battle was fought on Bloody Meadow in 1471 to end the Wars of the Roses.

When religious houses were being destroyed by Thomas Cromwell the townsfolk appealed for the ABBEY CHURCH to be spared, claiming it as their Parish church. Surprisingly their plea was heeded and they were allowed to buy it for £453.

Larger than many cathedrals its Norman tower dominates Tewkesbury, whilst the Nave is one of the most impressive sights in England. Interesting tombs include those of the De Clares, one of whom, Gilbert of 1314, fell at Bannockburn and his body was sent home for burial because his wife was sister to the wife of Robert Bruce!

The remains of the Duke of Clarence, drowned in a butt of Malmesbury wine, are here and there is a brass to Henry VI's only son whose body lay here after the Battle of Tewkesbury. So ghastly was that battle it is said the Abbey had to be cleansed and reconsecrated after it was over.

One of the Abbey treasures is an organ with a remarkable history. Built for Magdalen College, Oxford, about 1610 it was sent as a present to Cromwell at Hampton Court. There it is believed to have been played by his blind secretary John Milton. Known as The Milton Organ it has been loved by many people, and at least one ghost returns to the Abbey when it is played.

I was told about him by the Rev. Michael Seacombe, who wrote to me in 1983 from his vicarage in Barnwood, Gloucester:

"When I was assistant curate at TEWKESBURY ABBEY years ago, I heard various reports of ghosts seen there. The late Canon Brian Purefoy often mentioned the black monks and a grey lady he had seen, which of course tied up with the Benedictine foundation of the Abbey. No one seemed at all perturbed by them, but in my five years there I did not see any of them. One Sunday, though, a rather interesting incident occurred. A doctor whom I had met the previous year when he was on his way to Wales for a holiday, wrote to say he would be coming to the ABBEY again, so I invited him to lunch after the service. While my wife was in the kitchen getting the pudding he said,

"Do you know I saw a ghost in the Abbey this morning?"

"What sort of ghost? Where was it?

"A monk, in black, in the Lady Chapel".

That surprised me. He was a stranger to the area, yet his experience was similar to others I had been told about. On another occasion a visitor asked if I would demonstrate the Milton Organ during the lunch hour. The groundsman, a Canadian, was at the desk at the time, in charge of postcards and books, as well as the key to the organ chamber which I had to collect from him.

Asking the visitor to sit at the bottom of the CHURCH, I played the organ for about five minutes, then went to return the key. The grounds-man grinned, and in his strong Canadian voice remarked:

"Well, you sure shifted the ghosts!"

"Ghosts! What sort of ghosts?"

"A black monk. He passed between two of the pillars".

I heard that the ghosts were often active on the Feast of the Dedication. One evening, after dark, I spent some time in the ABBEY with a colleague and a local doctor, but nothing happened. Occasionally after dark, when the Abbey was closed, however, I used to play the organ and I thought I heard sounds. They may have been natural sounds, but all the same it was a bit eerie!"

I repeated this story some time later to a friend's husband, a Doctor of music, and was surprised when he replied: "I never play the organ in TEWKESBURY ABBEY after dark, nor in the village church at BISHOP'S CLEEVE, because I always have the feeling I am not alone".

Nearby Tewkesbury Abbey is St. Oswald's Gate where a monk used often to be seen by a nurse as she passed that way early in the morning.

Visitors leaving the Abbey can clearly see THE BELL HOTEL on the opposite side of the road. A beautiful half-timbered building it bears the date 1696, but this is thought to refer to a time of reconstruction as the style is of an earlier period. Mrs. Craik stayed there when she was writing John Halifax Gentlemen, and which she fictionalised as The Tanners House. Now her book is remembered by the naming of the John Halifax Penthouse Suite.

The present owner of THE BELL has not seen the ghost said to haunt the building, but he was very active a few years ago and alarmed some of the maids. Complaining that he interrupted their work they named him Henry but he is not bothering anyone at the moment.

From the front door of The Bell there is a good view of Abbey Mill in Mill Street, which Mrs. Craik names Abel Fletcher's Mill.

Abel Fletcher's mill and the River Avon

A few years ago two women, returning home late one night, were startled to see a coffin being carried along MILL STREET from the ABBEY towards St. Mary's Lane in a secretive manner. This is interesting because there used to be a burial ground in St. Mary's Lane. Unfortunately they did not make a note of the date as there has long been a legend of a midnight burial scene on May 7th, the coffin being carried near the Berkeley Arms. Maybe there is some connection, especially as the date of the Battle of Tewkesbury was May 4th.

During July or August 1982 a married couple drove from the village of Bishop's Cleeve to have a meal at The Bell Hotel and the wife wrote to tell me of the strange experience which befell them as they strolled along Church Street.

"It was late when we left THE BELL but it was still very hot and humid, so we decided to have a walk before driving home. Strolling towards the Cross we passed the Legion Club, which is opposite the Almshouses, and then ahead of us we saw two boys on crutches. They were about 8 and 12 years of age, and my first thought was one of surprise that they should be out so late. Then I realised how oddly they were dressed. The younger one was wearing old-fashioned grey knicker-bockers, fastened below his knees, and the elder one had a hooded coat, something like a duffle coat. In spite of the heat he had the hood up over his head, and he was wearing brown leather boots. Their crutches were old-fashioned too; they had arm pads on them, such as I had not seen since childhood.

Music was coming from the open windows of the Legion, and the boys started gaming about, trying to throw their crutches into the air, as if they were attempting to keep time to the music with their throwing. The elder boy suddenly turned, and seeing us they instantly scuttled down one of the alleys, or Courts as they're called in Tewkesbury.

Without a word we turned and hurried back to the car. When we got in I said to my husband, "I feel awful, as if I'd seen a ghost". "So do I," he said.

We drove home as quickly as we could, and although I think my husband put the boys out of his mind, I couldn't do that. I kept thinking about them and the strange look of them. A few weeks later I went over to Tewkesbury and talked to a young man I know who works in one of the shops. I asked if he had ever seen two crippled boys in the area. he had not and nor had the girl who worked with him. He told me, however, that the Court where the boys has disappeared led to the old Baptist Chapel and a graveyard.

Later I visited the Court with my husband. We looked into the very old Baptist Chapel, which had recently been renovated and refurbished, and then walked down the Court, past two timber framed cottages. They had been modernised and redecorated too, and looked most attractive. At the end of the Court an archway led to the old burial ground, (where a cast iron plaque bore the date 1655), which was bordered by a big wall, much too high for the boys to have climbed. I was perfectly sure, however, that they did not belong in either of those smart cottages, so where could they have gone?

I told the story to a close friend, and then came an unexpected sequel. In December 1982 she was invited to dine with some colleagues in Winchcombe, and knowing the man sitting next to her had lived in Tewkesbury she found herself telling him the story.

He listened attentively and when she had finished he said, "I didn't interrupt you as I wanted to hear the whole story. You see I was born in Tewkesbury fifty odd years ago, and three times in my lifetime I've heard exactly the same story. Unfortunately I've never been able to find out who those boys were".

Not satisfied to leave it there I did more research and learned that in medieval times three large timber framed hall houses were built along that Court. Standards changed over the years and eventually they were altered to provide what was probably the first Baptist Chapel in southern England, as well as a series of tiny cottages.

Since then numerous alterations have occurred, and at the turn of this century there were three tiny cottages in the Court, one consisting only of a single room.

Perhaps that was where the boys lived; such houses seem far more likely to have been their homes than the smart cottages which now exist in the Court"

Continuing along Church Street you will see a row of medieval buildings on the right, among them the John Moore Museum. John Moore was born in Tewkesbury and his account of life in the town in *Portrait of Elmbury*, the first book in the Brensham Trilogy, paints a vivid picture of life before the last war. It was appropriate that he should be buried under the shadow of the Abbey wall, facing the green sward which leads to the river.

THE ROYAL HOP POLE HOTEL is the next building to notice in Church Street. Thought to date from the 15th century it still retains some very attractive features, including a particularly charming dinning room. There is a garden too, running down to the river Avon where the hotel has private moorings; a very pleasant place to sit with a drink on a summer day.

Literary connections are proudly proclaimed by a plaque on the wall stating that "At the Hop Pole at Tewkesbury they stopped to Dine". The fare must have been good at that time too, because under the influence of combined stimulants Mr. Pickwick and Mr. Ben Allen fell fast asleep for thirty miles while Bob and Mr. Weller sang duets in the dickey.

Perhaps it is the ghost of Mr. Pickwick who has been seen by a porter early in the morning on a number of occasions sitting in a chair in "the square," a landing in the old part of the hotel, quietly enjoying his pipe.

Another porter, with a previous manager, saw a number of soldiers march across one of the bedrooms in the oldest part of the building, coming from one wall and disappearing through another. The manager described them as Roman soldiers because of the style of their uniforms and helmets, but no one on the present staff has seen them.

A soldier, fatally wounded on Bloody Meadow, crept into the HOP POLE after the battle, and since then his ghost is said to have walked in the bedroom where he died. A former manager, Mr. Derek Bailey, told an investigator in 1985 that several guests had seen him, but added, "I've got rather a soft spot for the chap. He's a pretty friendly phantom and part of the fixtures. I don't want him exorcised but he does not seem to have been seen lately.

If you want so see one of Tewkesbury's oldest, and perhaps most haunted pubs, THE BLACK BEAR, you will have to continue down Church Street to The Cross, and walk the length of High street, where you will find it on the corner.

In the 1930s it was taken over by a family named Beck, and shortly after they moved in, husband, wife, grown up son and daughter, were all awakened one night by a terrible commotion in the lounge below. Cries, groans, shouting and swearing echoed through the building, as well as the sound of hurrying footsteps.

Jumping out of their beds all four members of the family raced downstairs after their two barking dogs. Before they reached the foot of the stairs, however, the dogs came yelping back, tails between their legs, hair bristling. The noises ceased abruptly as the family neared the lounge door. Inside nothing had been disturbed and there were no signs of intruders. Puzzled, and a little afraid, the family searched the building but eventually decided to return to their beds. No sooner did they reach the top of the stairs than the noises began again. Father and son rushed back, but once again the noises stopped as they reached the lounge door. The family had little peace that night, but nothing untoward was discovered next day. The weeks which followed were quiet, but son John, who had never believed in ghosts, began doing some research and was startled to find the noises had occurred on the anniversary of the Battle of Tewkesbury in 1471. What was more, he learned that the lounge had been converted from the old stables, where, according to tradition, the wounded and dying had been brought after the battle on Bloody Meadow.

After that John saw other ghosts. One, a young man of gentle mien, garbed in black, his light brown hair cut in page-boy style, used to walk across a bedroom and disappear through the wall opposite. For what purpose no once could guess, but maybe he was making his way to Tewkesbury Abbey, for although no trace has been found a secret passage is believed to have linked the Black Bear with the Abbey.

One summer evening I was invited by the late Col. Blyth and his wife of Cheltenham to accompany them and other friends to the Black bear where we met John Beck. Five of us stood talking in what was then a central, stone flagged passage. From the public bar behind me came the hub-bub of cheerful voices and just before 10 o'clock a loud cry: 'Time gentlemen please! Time gentlemen please!'

We were not drinking and John, standing opposite to me, continued his conversation. Suddenly there was a loud hammering on the door behind him, which I was facing, and I saw the old-fashioned latch being jerked up and down. John glanced over his shoulder at it, then said to me, "What do you think that was?"

I laughed, "Some poor soul who'd arrived just too late for a drink I should think"

"What would you say if I told you that room is locked, there is no other door or window in it and the room is empty?"

"I wouldn't believe you John," I replied.

"Very well," he said, "All of you stay here and keep guard while I go and find a torch and the key"

I did not take my eyes off the door until John returned a few minutes later. Unlocking the door he escorted us all into a very small room. Shining his torch around I could see he was right; there was no other door or window.

"Walk over here," John said, guiding me to a circular hump in the floor.

"That was a well," he said, "And the story goes that when the stage coaches used to come through Tewkesbury, unwary travellers were coerced into this room to play cards. If they became difficult about losing money it was very easy to get rid of them down that well. Whether that's why we hear hammering on that door, and see the latch going up and down so violently I don't know, but I think it must be the ghost of some poor fellow who is still trying to get out of here."

Since then the building has been altered several times, so whether the ghost is still heard I do not know, but fairly recently there have been reports of a mysterious woman who sits alone in a corner. If anyone speaks to her she disappears into thin air. Sometimes she restlessly paces about, and she has also been seen lurking at the top of the stairs. Some say she is the ghost of a woman trampled beneath the flying hooves of a carriage horse many years ago, but there is no confirmation of the story. No one knows whether her appearance is anything to do with a strange occurrence experienced by several people a few years ago when, according to several eye-witnesses, heavy horseshoes hanging on the wall "flew across the room". There have been times when members of staff have refused to be alone in the pub. Who can blame them?

The Walk

Route: Abbey – Old Baptist Church – Abbey Mill – The Ham – High Street – Abbey.

Distance: 1³/₄ miles.

Terrain: Flat walking throughout, chiefly along town pavements. The Ham impassable at times of flood.

Finding Tewkesbury: Tewkesbury stands at the junction of the A38 and the A438, 10 miles north of Gloucester. O.S. Landranger Sheet 150 (Worcester and the Malverns).

Park and Start: Abbey car park, off Church Street (A38). GR 890325.

The Route

❑ From the ABBEY car park, turn left along the A38 (Church Street) and go over the pedestrian crossing. Watch for the narrow alley signposted to the OLD BAPTIST CHAPEL. After seeing this, and the graveyard adjoining, return to Church Street and turn right. THE BELL HOTEL is soon reached.

❑ Turn right alongside and follow MILL LANE towards Abbey Mill, noting the former Abbey tithe barn on the left.

❑ Cross the Mill Avon by the footbridge alongside Abbey Mill to enter the Ham.

❑ Those wishing to shorten the walk can do so by turning right and following the Mill Avon to the footbridge upstream. Otherwise follow the footpath straight over the Ham to reach the bank of the River Severn at a weir. Turn right along the river bank and follow the path as it swings to the right near the confluence of the Severn and the Avon. Continue to reach the footbridge spanning the Mill Avon.

❑ Cross and climb up to the High Street by any of the connecting streets or alleys. Beyond the Cross (War memorial) at the junction of the town's two main streets, watch for the ROYAL HOP POLE HOTEL on the right, with its 'plaque bearing a quotation from the 'Pickwick Papers'.

❑ The ABBEY and car park are soon reached on the left.

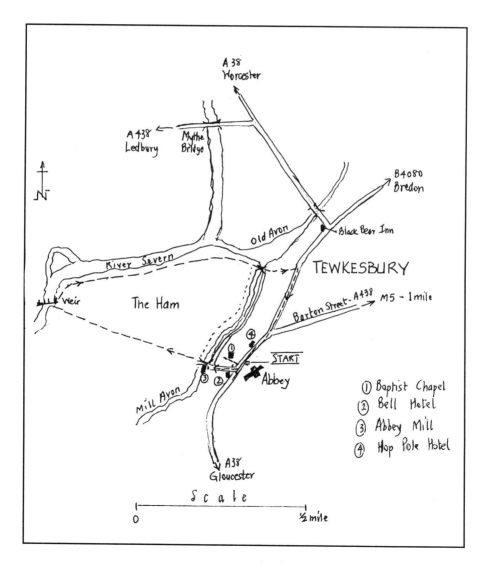

Points of Interest

Tewkesbury is an ancient town built at the meeting place of the rivers Severn and Avon. The massive tower of its magnificent Norman abbey dominates both the town and the surrounding countryside. This abbey is generally considered to be inferior only to Westminster Abbey and Beverley Minster among English churches without cathedral status.

Although close to the Cotswolds, Tewkesbury's allegiance lies with the Vale of Severn. Its streets are lined with an alluring mixture of timber-framed and red-brick buildings, many dating from the 16th, 17th and 18th centuries, and including several distinctive old inns and elegant town houses. On-foot exploration of the town is enhanced by the number of narrow alleyways, which provide intriguing glimpses into the nooks and crannies of old Tewkesbury that have survived the town's evolution from the 18th century milling, brewing and stocking-knitting centre to its modern state.

It is possible to take any number of interesting exploratory walks around Tewkesbury. The route included in this book was chosen because it passed several notable buildings as well as providing good views of the town from the Ham, an extensive water meadow managed in a traditional way. This involves a cycle of grazing during the winter months, followed by the growing of a hay crop, later sold by auction. In July, after hay-making, the grass is allowed to grow for a month, after which the aftermath, or right of pasturage, is also auctioned. Apart from the Abbey, the chosen walk passes four noteworthy buildings (numbered on the map):

1. **The Old Baptist Chapel and graveyard**, off Church Street, bears the date 1655. It is one of the oldest non-conformist chapels in Gloucestershire and is normally kept open for visitors to see the late 17th century furnishings.

2. **The Bell Hotel**, Church Street, is a gabled timber-framed building which was already old when re-built in 1696.

3. **Abbey Mill**, Mill Street, is early 19th century. The present building stands on the site of an earlier one by the Mill Avon (an artificial channel cut centuries ago to link the Avon with the Swilgate). The mill has a notable literary connection, featuring as Abel Fletcher's Mill in Mrs. Craik's Victorian novel, 'John Halifax Gentleman'.

4. **The Royal Hop Pole Hotel** also has its place in Victorian literature. As the plaque outside reminds us, Charles Dickens had Mr. Pickwick call here in his 'Pickwick Papers'. The hotel is an appealing mix of timber-framing and painted brick.

Half a mile to the south of the town centre, off Lincoln Green Lane, is Bloody Meadow, the site of the Battle of Tewkesbury, fought in 1471 by the victorious Yorkists under Edward IV against Queen Margaret's Lancastrians. A circular battle trail, waymarked by crossed swords on a rose motif, can be followed from the battle site, along Lower Lode and by the River Swilgate back to the start.

Those wishing to capture something of the atmosphere of early 20th century Tewkesbury can do no better than read the 'Brensham Trilogy' of books by local author John Moore (1907-1967).

Refreshments

The Bell Hotel, Opposite Abbey: Historic hotel. Accommodation; Restaurant; Refreshments throughout the day. Tel: 0684 293293.

Royal Hop Pole Hotel, Church Street: 15th century hotel; Accommodation; Restaurant; Bar meals; Garden running down to river Avon. Tel: 0684 293236.

The Black Bear, High Street: Ancient traditional Inn.

Gupshill Manor, Gloucester Road: Restaurant; Bar meals; Beer garden. Tel: 0684 292278.

Nearby Attractions:

Tewkesbury Abbey, Church Street: Beautiful Abbey and Gift Shop.

John Moore Countryside Museum, Church Street: Open Easter to October. Tuesday to Saturday and Bank Holidays – 10 am/1 pm; 2 pm/5 pm. Admission charge.

The Little Museum, Church Street: Easter to October – Tuesday to Saturday and Bank Holidays – 10 am/1 pm; 2 pm/5 pm.

Tewksbury Town Museum, 64 Barton Street: Easter to end October. Daily 10 am/1 pm; 2 pm/5 pm. Admission charge.

7

NEWENT

Newent is famed for its orchards and market gardens, as well as its long history. The town once boasted a Norman Priory and still retains the 16th century Market House, standing on posts, as well as many fine half-timbered buildings and a lovely church. Yet to many people the very name Newent conjures up pictures of vast areas of wild daffodils.

Now that it is forbidden to pick wild flowers, it is hard to remember that, even since the ending of the last war, special trains used to run from Cheltenham and other towns, packed with families going to Newent to pick the daffodils. In Cheltenham Gipsies used to wander along the Promenade, offering bunches of them for sale.

There is an old saying that "there are more ghosts in Gloucestershire than you can shake a stick at," and I did not expect any difficulty in collecting stories in Newent, but although helpful and kind the people there were not natural story tellers.

At the BLACK DOG HOTEL, for instance, there is a hint that the Black Dog may have had connections with Black Shuck of Over, but nothing more definite could be found.

As explained in another chapter, ghostly Black Dogs are legendary and sightings are reported from other countries as well as all parts of Britain. Some have eyes of fire and are threatening, but in England many appear to lonely travellers and walk with them, always on the left. They cannot be touched, (although there is a report of one which rubbed against the legs of a farmer, who said its skin seemed to be covered in bristles).

At the Black Dog at Newent, however, I could not find a definite story, and a letter to Whitbread's, the owners, drew a blank as their archives are being re-sited and historical records of pub names cannot be consulted at present. I did learn, however, that the friendly looking black dog on the Inn sign was not that of a ghost, but the portrait of a dog owned by one of Whitbread's directors.

Thanks to friendly staff at the Inn I was put in touch with Mr. Phil Biscoe, a local inhabitant, who told me something of the Inn's history. It was once a farmhouse, hence the reason why the 'front door' is at the side, and it is believed that King Charles was there at some time during the Civil War. Although there is no recent history of a ghost, years ago an Inn Keeper was upset when on two occasions, (both on June 16th), she saw an unhappy ghost in chains, but who he was, or the reason for his appearance, is not known.

A few yards from the BLACK DOG stands THE GEORGE HOTEL, a 17th century Coaching and Posting Inn, and here the landlord, Tony was able to tell me several stories. One night, at about 11 o'clock, he was sitting in the lounge with a group of visitors when they heard the sound of horses' hooves and wheels clattering over the cobblestones in the yard. His mother was upstairs, but she came down and said, "Did you hear the coach arrive?" which of course they had. One of the top rooms at the hotel is reputed to be haunted by a chamber maid and Tony took me up to see it. We stepped through a door which opened at one end of a short corridor. There were two rooms on each side of the corridor, and blocking off the far end of it was a door leading into a bathroom.

In the summer of 1992, an Australian visitor booked into the hotel and was given one of these rooms. He was the only guest up there.

During the early house he arose to go to the bathroom. As he came out of it, sleepily fastening his pyjamas, he was embarrassed to find himself facing a woman. Hastily withdrawing back into the bathroom he adjusted his pyjamas and re-emerged to find the corridor empty.

Next morning he went in search of Tony to apologise, explaining that he thought he was alone up there. Tony assured him he had been, and finally took him into the dining room to see the only other woman there, whom the Australian agreed was not the one he had seen.

Tony put me in touch with another local resident, a Mr. Larkworthy, from whom I learned that buildings known as BLACK DOG COTTAGES are reputed to be haunted, and that there is a Black Dog Lane at the back of The George but nearby is CLEEVE MILL LANE, and this is the one he heartily dislikes.

"It's about a mile long," he told me, "But I'd rather walk four miles than go along there at night. I always have an uneasy, cold feeling there. I think I must be psychic."

Perhaps he is because of an unusual experience he had at a house called STARDENS, near the By-pass. Once a private house it became a Country Club for a time, but is now privately owned again.

While it was a Country Club Mrs. Larkworthy worked there as a cook. "One night," Mr. Larkworthy said, "I was in the Bar with several others, including Chris, the owner's son. Suddenly I saw a very beautiful woman coming down the stairs. She was wearing a green, crinoline type dress, and I watched her turn along the passage and go out through the front door. I asked who she was and I was amazed to find no one else had seen her. They all thought it was a great joke, but I knew I'd seen her.

Sometime afterwards I was shown a picture of a former owner of STARDENS, a Mrs. Onslow, and I recognised her immediately. She was the woman I had seen coming down the stairs."

Stardens, I understand, stands near the by-pass, but when the next story was sent to me by Mrs Chandler-Powell of Newent the exact site was not given. This is what she wrote:

"As a child of nine I lived in a haunted house. Nothing was ever actually seen, but there was a definite 'presence'. For the first time in my life I became afraid of the dark and would not go up to bed unless my mother or father accompanied me, and in one room, which housed the piano where I was supposed to practice, I was always uncomfortable and felt as though I was being watched by unseen eyes.

Our dog, a fierce Airedale, firmly refused to enter that room. If any of us were in it he'd lie outside the door whimpering. On one or two occasions when we tried to get him inside, his hackles rose and he fled howling. One night there was a terrific sound of breaking glass, and we thought a stone had been thrown through the greenhouse, but on inspection there was absolutely nothing to be seen.

We moved after a year and later discovered that a notoriously evil man had one lived there who was suspected of murdering his wife, though this was not proved as her body was never found. Afterwards he had drowned himself."

Perhaps that kind of haunting is understandable, but the next one was more puzzling and worried Richard Yates, who sent it to me, because he did not believe in ghosts!

"Years ago," he wrote, "I was engaged to a girl who lived in Hereford, whom I used to visit at weekends. When I drove down I would take my mother as far as Dymock where she stayed with my aunt and cousin, and I picked her up again on my return journey on Sunday.

It was usually pretty late when we left Dymock, and one Sunday it was close to midnight as we drove towards the steep, hump-backed bridge at GREENWAY HALT which used to cross the old railway line between Ledbury and Newent, where we both saw a man crossing the road. He was wearing a pale coat, which could have been a raincoat. He came through the hedge on one side of the road, crossed to the other and disappeared through that hedge. I jokingly remarked to my mother,

"I bet he's stealing someone's chickens!', and we thought no more about him.

A week later, however, when we came round a bend approaching the bridge there he was again, and I had to brake hard to miss him. I thought he must be a tramp because there were no houses anywhere near. But I was puzzled as to what he was up to, and made up my mind to investigate in daylight the next week. To my surprise I found that not only were there no openings in the hedge, from which he had emerged, but strands of wire would have made it impossible for anyone to step through.

Wondering if it could be a trick of the light reflected off the tarmac, I positioned myself at dusk one evening, when the roads were wet, with the car headlights in every conceivable position, but I could not find a clue. Finally I concluded that it had been a patch of mist crossing the road, which, by coincidence, I had come across twice.

Two days later, when my mother was in the car, we both saw the figure again! It is the one time in my whole life when I have felt chilling fear. I felt prickling sensation at the back of my neck, and I was very frightened!

I advised my mother not to say anything to her sister, and I kept the story to myself because I thought people would question my sanity. About a year ago, however, my mother started telling the story to her sister, and then, to our astonishment, we discovered that my cousin had twice seen a similar figure on that bridge!

None of the three of us is mad, or even strange! We are all completely normal and I don't believe in ghosts . . . but such a thing had been seen without any shadow of doubt!"

Perhaps it was harder on Richard Yates than on most people because he did not believe in ghosts, but while you ponder his story, as the walk today is short, perhaps you will be inclined to wander along the Dymock Road towards Pauntley Court, for this was once the home of the Whittington family, the most famous member being Sir Richard, known to most of us as Dick Whittington.

The Walk

Route: Car park – Market Hall – Church – Lake – By-pass – Car park.

Distance: 1¹/₄ miles.

Terrain: Level throughout, apart from lakeside section of route which is mainly along town pavement.

Finding Newent: Newent lies at the junction of the B4215 and the B4216 nine miles North-West of Gloucester. O.S. Landranger Sheet 163 (Gloucester and Forest of Dean).

Park and Start: Free car park off Broad Street. GR 722260.

The Route

❑ Leave the car park along the no-through-road to the right of the main entrance.

❑ At a T-junction, go right to reach Broad Street, opposite the Market hall.

❑ Turn left along Church Street, passing the GEORGE HOTEL on the right, to reach the church-yard of St. Mary the Virgin. (Visit to the church strongly recommended).

❑ THE BLACK DOG INN is further along the street on the right.

❑ Go through the church-yard and turn left to reach the lake via a barrier at the end of a road. Follow the path to the right round the lake (i.e. in an anti-clockwise direction).

❑ After completing the circuit, turn right up a surfaced path (known locally as Old Maids Walk). Cross an estate road to reach the top of High Street near its junction with the B4215 (Newent by-pass). A short way to the right along this road, and on the opposite side, is a plaque marking the site of the Gloucester-Hereford Canal (1796-1883) and the Gloucester-Hereford Railway (1883-1964).

❑ Return to the start along High Street. The car park is on the left.

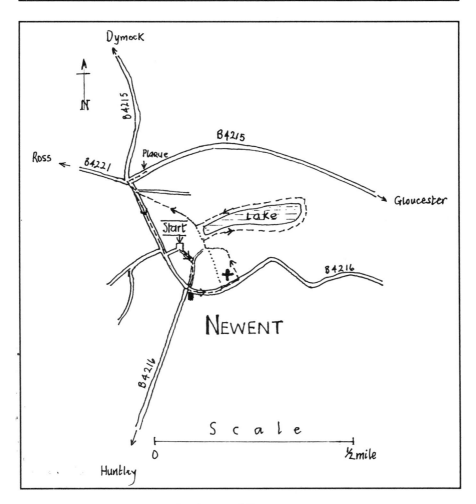

Points of Interest

The largest centre of population in North-west Gloucestershire, Newent is an ancient place that owed its importance in the medieval period largely to its position on one of the main drovers' roads from Wales.

Evidence of the town's existence in pre-Conquest times can be seen in the porch of the parish church. This is in the form of part of the shaft of a 9th century Saxon cross, four centuries older then the church itself, the

153 feet high spire of which dominates the town. This is in fact the second spire, the first having been blown down by a gale in 1661. Soon afterwards, in 1674, the roof of the nave collapsed shortly after the congregation had left Sunday evening service. The fine replacement nave is the work of local craftsmen, using among other materials 80 tons of Forest of Dean timber supplied by Charles II.

Newent market hall

Perhaps Newent's most distinctive building is the timber-framed Market Hall, standing on sixteen oak pillars and dating from 1668. Built as a butter market, this handsome structure once commanded the busy market square, a scene of great activity when Newent served as the trading centre of the Vale of Leadon. Between the Market Hall and the church is the Shambles Museum, an intriguing complex of streets and alleys hidden from view by the Victorian houses lining the street. Close by are two interesting inns, The George, once an important coaching establishment, and The Black Dog, partly timber-framed and formerly a farmhouse.

Newent Lake, a delightful amenity, belonged formerly to the Court, a substantial Georgian mansion demolished in 1970. It was created from fish-ponds associated with the long-disappeared Newent Priory. The footpath around the Lake provides excellent views of ducks, coots and moorhens, together with a variety of tits and finches in the tops of the surrounding trees.

At the eastern end of the lake can be seen part of the dried-up bed of the former Hereford and Gloucester Canal, which closed in 1883 after 87 years service. Another reminder of this lost waterway, and of the railway which succeeded it before itself closing in 1964, can be seen alongside the town by-pass (B4215) near the end of the walk. This is a plaque, inserted into the rock face by the Gloucestershire Society for Industrial Archaeology.

Refreshments

The George Hotel, Church Street: 17th century coaching Inn; Accommodation; Package and weekend breaks. Open all day. Bar and evening meals. Tel: 0531 820203.

The Black Dog, Church Street: Whitbread Hotel; Cavalier Bar; Bar meals. Open 11 am/2 pm. Tel: 0531 821012.

Nearby Attractions:

The Shambles Museum, Church Street: Depicts Victorian life. Open March/December – 10 am/ 6 pm. Closed Mondays except Bank Holidays. Gift Shop; Lunches; Teas.

National Birds of Prey Centre, Cliffords Mesne, Nr. Newent: Largest private collection of birds of prey in Europe. Gift and bookshop; Coffee Shop; Picnic area. Tel: 0531 820286

Butterfly and Natural World Centre, Springbank, Birches Lane, Newent: Tropical butterflies, insect gallery, reptiles. Tel: 0531 821800.

8

GLOUCESTER – A CITY WALKABOUT

Gloucester is a busy, bustling city and those who hurry through could be forgiven for not realising this is a very ancient place.

Gloucestershire has been an important area of Britain since before the Romans marched in. There is a local saying "Scratch Gloucestershire and you'll find Rome" but there is much else besides, and the city of Gloucester has been the scene of many stirring events.

Myths and legend are inextricably mixed. Tales are still told of the long siege during the Civil War, and of how the city was saved by a pig. Faced with starvation inside the city walls surrender seemed inevitable on the day when only one pig remained to feed the inhabitants.

Outside the walls lay the troops, knowing food must be getting scarce, waiting for the surrender. But the people were resourceful and a plan was concocted. The pig was to be led around the inside of the walls, and as he was trotting along his snout was to be repeatedly pinched.

The poor thing screamed in terror, again and again, and the troops outside listened in amazement, convinced that after all there was plenty of food inside the walls. Surrender was unlikely, they thought, and so they withdrew.

King Charles had his revenge later when he ordered the demolition of the city walls, gates and castle, and so only the names of the streets are there to remind us of them.

It is not necessary to look far for historic buildings, however, and ghosts which haunt them. At THE CROSS KEYS, an ancient inn to be found in Cross keys Lane, there is a ghost whom some would call mischievous, whilst others would consider him difficult.

According to the Innkeeper's wife, Stella Gaston, his name is Eroso, a Spaniard beheaded in the city about 1760 when he was 35 years old. He claimed to have been buried somewhere on the site of the Inn, and to have been put to death because he was a lecher. Certainly he seems to like the company of female members of staff, and though few are afraid of him they get annoyed when he plays tricks, such as turning the heat down when Yorkshire puddings are being cooked. Once the beer became frothy when pump pressure gauges had been tampered with, although a special key is needed to adjust them.

Sometimes, he steals things the staff are using, such as spoons or knives and returns them days later when they are not needed. Lights go on and off and sometimes taps won't work; then staff get annoyed and tell him to "Stop messing about!"

A new cleaner became upset on her first day when her bucket kept hovering about, but Stella reassured her by telling her not to be afraid as he would not touch her. That, says Stella, is something she would not accept!

When she plans any change, even putting up new pictures, she tells Eroso what she is going to do, "and then he doesn't mind," but when a workman was called in, and started drilling a wall without doing so, Eroso pulled his trousers down! The man came rushing out and refused to return to finish the work.

Eroso likes one end of the Bar and some members of staff do not like working there in the early morning.

If you find your way into THE CROSS KEYS, Stella will be willing to talk about Eroso, especially if you happen to be historians who can add to the information she has already gleaned from the Archives about the history of the Inn.

There is a different kind of ghost in Gloucester PRISON, one of the few haunted ones in Britain. Although the inmates have usually been men, the ghost is that of a woman, Jenny Godfrey, who it is believed was murdered in a cell in the 15th century. There were rumours of a haunted cell and of furniture being moved around by unseen hands for some time, but in 1969 some of the prisoners held a seance and claimed to have communicated with Jenny.

After that there was a considerable amount of disturbance in the cells, when books and other objects were thrown about, as well as odd noises. Whether they still occur it has not been possible to ascertain.

Jenny, like Eroso at The Cross Keys, had died a violent death, but there are other kinds of ghosts too. A lady who had lived in a Victorian house in Gloucester for a number of years, told me she opened her cellar door one day and was startled to find herself face to face with a Roman soldier.

"I was too surprised to be afraid," she said, "And he looked startled too, then just disappeared in front of my eyes."

Someone else in the city wrote to me:

"After I became a widow I was alarmed by burglaries in the district where I live. One night I awoke suddenly to find a man by my bed and thought it was a burglar. I could see clearly by the light of street lamps outside, but was afraid at first to look up to his face. My heart was beating furiously as I raised my eyes above his waist level and found myself staring at my husband, standing in characteristic attitude and looking just as he did when he was young. He looked well and oh so real! As I gazed up at him he slowly faded from my sight, but I felt no fear – he was alive and well."

Monks are to be found in most historic cities and it is not surprising to find one at BLACKFRIARS PRIORY. A few years ago workmen were alarmed when they saw him, and they complained they could not always get into their huts because doors became mysteriously locked.

The New Inn

One of the most attractive historic buildings in the city is the NEW INN, Northgate Street, its galleried courtyard festooned with greenery. Rebuilt in 1455 it housed pilgrims to the shrine of Edward II; Elizabethan plays were performed there and it is believed the document proclaiming Lady Jane Grey as Queen of England was read from the gallery.

One of the bedrooms is named after

her, but the room favoured by the ghost, which leads off the far end of the gallery, is known as the Oak Suite.

A large four poster bed stands in the panelled room, which is haunted by a man who "likes the ladies".

Marian Thomas, a member of staff at the Inn for a number of years, told me it is women guests who mostly complain of disturbance in the room. One of the receptionists, the possessor of strong nerves, decided to spend two nights in the room to find out for herself what happened.

The first night she found the blankets were so tightly pulled around her that she could not move, but on the second night she was not disturbed.

When a Psychic Fair was held in the hotel, a medium was taken to see the room, but not told anything about the ghost. She described a man of scruffy appearance lying on the bed, who, she said, had died of an 'unpleasant disease'.

No one has seen him, but maids always like to leave the door open when they are cleaning the room.

Marian took me to see the delightful low beamed dining room. At the far end is an area which seems to have been added on to the original room. This was once a Staff room, but there is a chill feeling and no one liked using it.

When one of the waitresses was in the Bar one day she saw a figure in a dark suit, carrying a brief-case, enter the Wine Press, but there was no one to be found and no way for anyone to get out.

Whether you hope to see a ghost or not, the NEW INN is a fascinating building, well worth a visit.

Not far away, in Westgate Street, stands another old inn, THE FLEECE, founded in the 15th century to house some of the many pilgrims flocking to the city. Only two of many such hostelries became established as "Great Inns" the Fleece being one of them. Not many ghosts are to be seen, although the figure of a Grey lady, probably of the Tudor period has been seen going up the stairway, then disappearing into the wall, as if walking through it.

A Victorian landlord has also been seen, and the manager described a strange incident which occurred a few years ago when a man who had applied for a job at the inn was accommodated there for the night before the interview.

He locked his door before going to bed, but rushed out next morning, greatly agitated, declaring that although his door was still locked his clothes and belongings had been turned upside down.

The manager confirmed that everything was in a state of disarray. Not surprisingly the man did not accept the job at the hotel.

Before leaving I was taken down to see the huge stone vaulted crypt beneath the hotel, known as the Monk's Retreat. Built in the 12th century its origin is a mystery. One theory is that it was a charnel house for the church of St. Mary de Grace which stood nearby in Westgate Street; another that it was used as a chapel. What is known, however, is that after the establishment of the Great Inn above there was close association with the Benedictine monks of St. Peter's Abbey, and a belief that the vault was joined by an underground passage to the Abbey.

The walls and pillars lean outwards, and no one knows whether this is the way they were built, or whether the stonework is without proper foundations and that pressure over the years has caused the walls to sink and spread.

It is the sort of place one would expect to be haunted, but there are no ghostly tales to be told. The strange medieval look of the place, however, is well worth seeing and that is possible if you are so inclined as it is used as a bar and so open to the public on Friday and Saturday evenings.

In Westgate Street, not far from The Fleece, there is a story of a modern ghost, told to me by Mr. Larkworthy of Newent. "When I was a young man," he told me, "I went to work at BURTOL'S, the Cleaners, on a site where there is now a building society. There was another chap working with me, but no one else in the building. He poured out two cups of tea, but before drinking them we went to pull clothes out of the driers. We were only away two or three minutes, but when we got back, the cups had disappeared. We couldn't make head or tail of it. Then we heard a woman upstairs calling her husband. I've never been so scared in my life. We knew there was nobody there. We took to our heels I can tell you and neither of us ever went back."

Finally, at the end of your walk, you will return to the CATHEDRAL, where, according to another legend, Little Tommy Tucker once sang in the choir.

No doubt you will stay a while to look at the treasures in the Cathedral, including its great East Window, "the size of a tennis court" the Cathedral architect one told me. A monk is said to walk here, but although I spent many hours working as a Helper in the Cathedral, I never sensed his presence, nor felt the eerie sensation sometimes experienced in Tewkesbury Abbey.

The last story I have to tell, however, is not of a ghost, yet it warrants a place here for it is a strange tale of dreams foretelling the future for the famous organist, Sir Herbert Brewer.

The story was sent to me by Miss Cramp, of Bromsgrove, whose father had been a friend of Sir Herbert.

"While at Tonbridge in 1896 Sir Herbert heard that the organistship at Liverpool Town Hall was vacant, and he applied for it. After hearing he had been chosen, with two others, to compete for the post, he had a vivid dream that his organist friend Lee Williams was retiring from GLOUCESTER CATHEDRAL. This was the place, above all others, where Sir Herbert wished to work, so when the dream occurred on three successive nights, he wrote to Liverpool asking to withdraw his application.

His friends, not knowing why he had taken such action, told him he was a fool and urged him to think again. Losing confidence in view of the criticism he sent a telegram to the Town Clerk of Liverpool asking to be allowed to withdraw his letter of resignation.

A telegram came back informing him that another candidate's name had been inserted in place of his, but that the matter would be put before a special committee. Evidently Sir Herbert was a strong candidate because the committee allowed him to withdraw his letter. Immediately he had his dream again! It was so very strong that he again wired the Town Clerk asking for his name to be removed from the list of applicants!

There is no record of the comments of Town Clerk or committee, but he received a terse reply: "Have definitely withdrawn your name."

If Sir Herbert had any more doubts, however, he did not have to wait long, because a month later the organistship of Gloucester Cathedral became vacant through the resignation of his friend Lee Williams on account of ill-health.

Sir Herbert applied and on December 15th 1896 the Gloucester Citizen announced his appointment as organist of Gloucester cathedral. He was well loved there and fondly remembered – all because of a dream.

The Walk

Route: Cathedral – St. Mary's Square – Millers Green – Northgate Street – The Cross – Cross Keys Lane – Bull Lane – Longsmith Street – Barbican Way – The Quay – The Docks – Ladybellgate Street – Blackfriar – Southgate Street – Westgate Street – College Court – Cathedral.

Distance: $2^1/_2$ miles.

Terrain: Along level pavements and walkways throughout.

Finding Gloucester: Gloucester is at the junction of the A38, A40 and A417.

Park and Start: Outside the main entrance to the Cathedral. O.S. Landranger Sheet 162 (Gloucester and Forest of Dean). GR 831188. Choice of official car parks.

The Route

❑ Facing the main entrance to the CATHEDRAL, turn left and walk round College Green and through St. Mary's Gate into St. Mary's Square. Retrace steps through the Gate and turn left into Millers Green. Continue as far as a signpost indicating 'Cathedral via Gardens' on the right. Keep left along Cathedral Way (Via Sacra) to reach Northgate Street via St. John's Lane.

❑ Turn right and follow Northgate Street to the Cross, passing the NEW INN on the left. Keep straight on along Southgate Street as far as the narrow Cross Keys Lane on the right. This leads via Bull Lane to Longsmith Street. Go left down Barbican Road and follow the sign on the right leading to the PRISON.

❑ Now keep left to reach the Quay. Cross with care and turn left. On reaching Severn Road, do not cross the bridge but follow the Mariners' Walk sign into the Docks.

❑ After exploring the Docks, leave through the gateway to the left of the one entered earlier. Cross Commercial Road and turn right to reach Ladybellgate Street on the left. Follow this as far as BLACKFRIARS on the right and continue to reach Southgate Street once more.

❑ Turn left and continue back to the Cross. Here, turn left into Westgate Street, passing the FLEECE INN on the left. Turn right along College Court, passing through St. Michael's Gateway and back on to College Green.

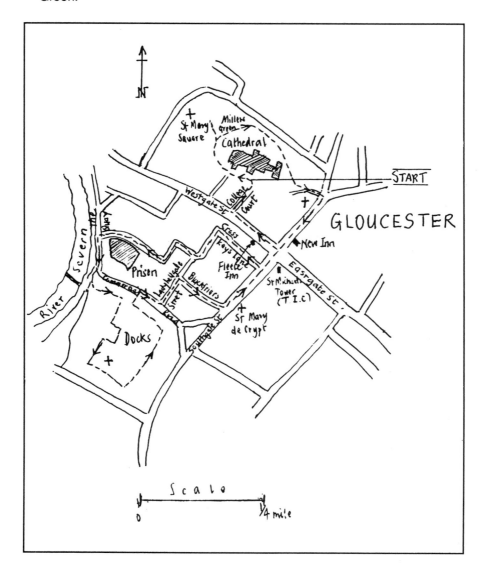

St Mary's Gate

Points of Interest

Gloucester came into being as the Roman military centre of *Glevum*, built to command the River Severn and to serve as the gateway to Wales. By the end of the Roman invasion, the city was one of the four great Coloniae of Britain, with walls enclosing homes, temples and a forum.

The grid of Roman streets, or gates, still comprises the city's basic layout and the intersection of these, known as the Cross, remains the hub of the modern city.

Despite an appalling amount of demolition of historic old buildings, and their replacement with much uninspiring property after the Second World War, Gloucester still boasts many fine buildings. Outstanding is of course the Cathedral, which towers majestically over the city and ranks among the country's finest. Begun in the 11th century as a Saxon monastery, St. Peter's consists of a Norman core with 14th century additions, including superb cloisters, transepts and choir.

Within can be seen the ornate tomb of the murdered King Edward II, which later became a shrine to which pilgrims flocked. Created a cathedral after the dissolution of the monasteries, St. Peter's shelters remnants of monastic buildings. These include St. Mary's Gate (leading to the Victorian memorial to the martyred Bishop Hooper) and vestiges of others in Miller's Green.

Other distinctive old buildings passed on the route of the walk include a delightful group of 17th and 18th century houses on College Green, King's School House, Blackfriars, parts of which date from the 13th century, and the restored Norman church of St. Mary de Crypt on Southgate Street.

Several interesting old inns also feature on the walk, The most appealing is perhaps the timber-framed New Inn, said to have been built for the use of pilgrims by John Twyning, a monk from the nearby abbey, in about 1450. It is notable for its galleried courtyard. The Fleece, too, claims 15th century origins, although its undercroft, now known as the Monk's Retreat, is believed to date from the 12th century.

By contrast, Gloucester prison is of comparatively recent origin, having been built on the site of the former castle in 1790. The building has been enlarged and modernised several times.

Gloucester Docks were built to promote trade along the River Severn between Bristol and the Midlands. Gloucester had been granted port status by Elizabeth I in 1580 but it was the cutting of the canal from Sharpness, on the Severn Estuary, in 1827 that brought trade and prosperity to the city. Today the restored docks are the home of the

National Waterways Museum, with the giant 19th century warehouses converted into a variety of uses for visitors. Close by stands an early Victorian mariners' church.

Refreshments

The New Inn, Northgate Street: Built in 1350 to house pilgrims, then rebuilt in 1455. Galleried Courtyard; Accommodation; Restaurant; Bar meals. Tel: 0452 522177.

The Fleece Hotel, Westgate Street: Historic hotel, trading as a Great Inn since 1534. Accommodation and restaurant. Tel: 0452 522762.

The Cross Keys, Cross Keys Lane, Gloucester: Claims to be the oldest pub in Gloucester. Bar meals with fresh vegetables. Listed in Good Beer Guide. Open 11 am/11 pm.

Nearby Attractions

Gloucester Cathedral: Strikingly beautiful building and crypt. Gift Shop and cafe.

Gloucester City Museum and Art Gallery, Brunswick Road: Open Monday/Saturday except at Christmas, New Year and Good Friday.

House of the Tailor of Gloucester, 9 College Court: Chosen by Beatrix Potter as setting for story of the Tailor of Gloucester. Bookshop selling her books, toys etc.

Gloucester Folk Museum, 99-103 Westgate Street: Open Monday/ Saturday – 10 am/ 5 pm. Closed Christmas, New Year and Good Friday.

Gloucester Docks: Several museums including the National Waterways; Robert Opie Collection, etc. Admission charge.

9

FRAMPTON-ON-SEVERN

Frampton's Magnificent Green, claimed to be the largest in the country, provides the perfect setting for a legendary story of the love of a king for a commoner more then 800 year's ago.

Jane Clifford, daughter of William de Clifford, was born about 1140 in the 'bower' of Frampton Manor, and was renowned for her beauty. Henry II is said to have met her on the banks of the river and to have fallen in love with her. She became his *Rosa muni*, his rose of the world, and to this day the village green is known as Rosamund's Green.

She became Henry's mistress and is thought to have had two children by him. Mystery surrounded her death in 1177 and there was some suspicion that she had been poisoned by Queen Eleanor.

There have been Cliffords in Frampton on Severn since 1081 when they were granted lands by William the Conqueror. Only the bower remains from the 12th century Manor, and FRAMPTON COURT, dating from 1732, is now the family home of Mrs. Henriette Clifford who told me that she remembers, as a child, hearing the sound of very heavy footsteps ascending two flights of back stairs. Others heard them too, but they have not been heard for a long time now. Her governess also saw an elderly lady, in old fashioned clothes, on the stairs in the entrance hall, and in recent years a visitor to the house has also seen a similar figure there although no one knows who she is. There were few other reports of ghosts in the village, however, until an elderly American lady came to live at DE LACY COTTAGE and, to her surprise, discovered she had the ability to step into the past.

Her son, Dan Phillips, moved into this cottage with his wife in 1984. There were no unusual happenings until his mother Beatrice came to live with them. One day, shortly after her arrival, whilst sitting reading in the sitting room she realised a woman was standing facing the fireplace, and the room somehow looked different. As the woman turned, Beatrice saw that she looked very ill.

She was not alarmed but puzzled and when neighbours were told they recognised the description as that of a former owner of the cottage, who had died after a long illness; after her death the cottage had been altered. On another occasion Beatrice was walking home to the cottage when she was surprised to see someone working in the garden. She first thought it must be her daughter-in-law, but as she drew near she could see the woman was wearing clothes of the Puritan period. Once, when Beatrice and her daughter-in-law were in the kitchen preparing tea for visitors, they heard footsteps outside. Looking out of the window Beatrice saw people passing clad in strange clothes of harsh shades of blue and red,; she asked Dan if there were hippies in the village, but that evening the *Gloucester Citizen* reported that it was the anniversary of the mustering on The Green of the Frampton Regulars, formed to repulse any Napoleonic invaders who might come up the Severn. Outfitted by Nathaniel Winchcombe, Lord of Frampton Court, the description of their uniforms given in the Citizen tallied with those described by Beatrice.

On another occasion she saw a Roman soldier, with shield and helmet, walk across the garden, and an elderly Edwardian type man looked out of the COTTAGE window. The little white dog with hair over its eyes, which she often saw, was remembered by neighbours as it had lived at the Cottage and had been buried in the garden.

Frampton-on-Severn, the church

Somehow, after coming to England, Beatrice had developed a gift for looking into the past, a gift she did not understand, but one which delighted her.

Maybe you too will sense something of the past as you wander around this lovely village. If you have time to visit the church, take a look at the door, with its antique lock and huge key, then run your hand over the surface of the door and feel its strange covering. Tradition has it that it is covered with the skin of wild boar which once roamed in this region.

The Walk

Route: The Street – Church – Splatt Bridge – The Green – Canal – The Street.

Distance: $2^1/_2$ miles.

Terrain: Level walking throughout, along minor roads and field paths, which may be muddy after rain.

Finding Frampton: Frampton on Severn lies on the B4071, and is two miles NW of the A38-A419 junction and 10 miles SW of Gloucester. O.S. Landranger Sheet 162 (Gloucester and Forest of Dean).

Park and Start: Near the phone box on The Street, the continuation of the road alongside The Green. GR 746075.

The Route

❏ From the phone box, continue along THE STREET (i.e. away from the Green) and go through the lychgate leading towards the church. This is reached along a footpath between horse chestnut trees.

❏ Pass the church and churchyard on the left and cross a stile in a fence to follow a grassy path and reach the canal tow-path over a stiled footbridge.

❏ Turn left to reach Splatt Bridge.

❏ From the bridge, turn left along the road towards the village.

❏ Immediately beyond a left hand bend, cross a stile on the right by a power pole and follow a public footpath to reach a T-junction of paths.

❏ Turn left. Cross the end of a road, go over a stile, and continue between lakes. Cross another stile and passing beached boats on the right, follow a fence on the right, keeping parallel to a service road as far as a stile.

❏ Cross and turn left along the road back to the village street.

❏ Cross and turn right along the edge of the Green. Opposite the end of a large pond, and immediately beyond Old Manor Farm, follow a public footpath signposted 'Frampton Bridge'. Cross three stiles and a footbridge and keep right round the edge of a field.

❑ Just before reaching the canal, follow the waymark to the left along the field edge to follow the canal, passing eventually through bushes to reach a stile in a hedge immediately beyond a grassy track crossing the path.

❑ Cross the stile and follow a zig zag path across a long field to reach a stile at the far end, leading to a lane.

❑ Continue along the lane to reach THE STREET and the start.

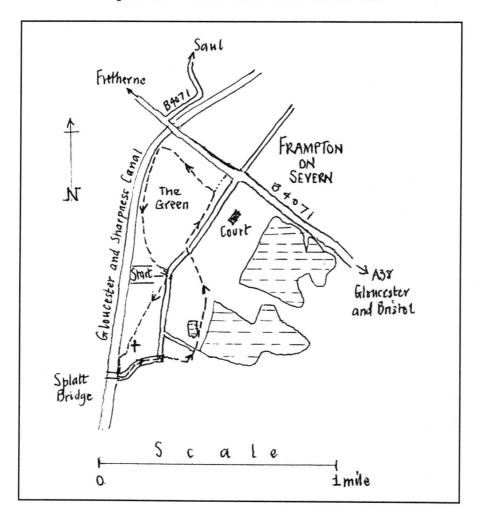

Points of Interest

Three miles or so up river from Slimbridge, of Wildfowl and Wetland Trust fame, Frampton on Severn lies inland from the river from which it takes its name. Between the village and the Severn is the Sharpness and Gloucester Canal, while inland is a complex of flooded gravel pits, which form a miniature water park and serve as a valuable wildfowl refuge.

Frampton is one of the most elegant villages, not only in the Severn Vale, but arguably in the whole of Gloucestershire. Its most striking feature is the 22-acre village green, the largest in the county and beautifully maintained, with rush-fringed ponds and avenues of horse chestnut trees.

The name of Clifford has a centuries-old link with Frampton. In the parish church can be seen splendid effigies of early members of the family, including one of William Clifford, dressed as a knight in armour, his feet resting on a dog, and one of his wife, complete with wimple and gown.

During the early 19th century other Cliffords left their mark in a different way. As was revealed in 1985 by the publication of 'The Frampton Flora', the extensive collection of flower paintings by the 'Clifford ladies' comprise a remarkable artistic achievement that amazingly lay forgotten in an attic at Frampton Court for well over a century.

The grace of Frampton's green is matched by that of its buildings. As well as its fine 14th century church, historic manor farm house and elegant 18th century Court, the village contains a richly diverse assortment of inns, cottages, farms and barns in which Cotswold slates mingle with mellow red pantiles and thatch, red brick harmonises with weathered stone, and vast wooden beams are evident in generous measure.

The Sharpness and Gloucester Canal adds further interest. Sixteen miles long and 90 feet wide, it was opened in 1827 and was the largest in the country until the construction of the Manchester Ship Canal. Its building almost halved the distance boats had to travel to reach Gloucester and it was designed to carry vessels of up to 1,000 tons. At Splatt Bridge can be seen one of the distinctive bridge-keeper's cottages, complete with elegant Doric columns.

Refreshments

The Bell Hotel, Frampton on Severn: Traditional country Inn.

Three Horse Shoes, Frampton on Severn: Traditional country Inn.

Nearby Attractions

Frampton Court, Frampton on Severn: Open to parties by appointment. Holiday accommodation in Orangery. Resident owner Mrs. Peter Clifford. Tel: 0452 740267.

St. Mary's Church: Mainly 14th century. Stone effigies of Clifford Crusaders.

St. Augustine's Farm, Arlingham (off A38): Families welcome. Open Wednesday/Sunday and Bank Holidays – 12 noon to 6 pm. Tel: 0452 740277. Admission charge.

Frampton Old Manor Farm

10

ULEY AND OWLPEN

History and beauty intermingle throughout Gloucestershire but in this area there is spectacular scenery and a staggering wealth of archeological remains, including a number of important Iron Age settlements.

It was difficult to know where to begin and the walk starts two miles from Dursley so the ghosts there must wait for another book, but it is worth noting that advertisements for The Old Bell Hotel there include the words: "Ask about our resident ghosts – they're quite harmless".

There is a legend that another Inn once stood high on the hills between DURSLEY and STROUD. Long ago, on a winter's day, a lonely horseman set off to ride over these hills to Stroud, but snow began to fall and he made slow progress. The light failed, the cold grew intense as snowflakes blinded his vision. Struggling on, his horse stumbling and slipping, he realised at last that he was lost. To be out in a blizzard on such a night was a terrifying thought, and then, as if in answer to his prayers, he saw the glimmer of a lamp somewhere ahead of him. Urging on his tired horse, sometimes blinded by the snowflakes, somehow he managed to keep going, to discover to his delight that the lamp was shining from the windows of an Inn.

As he drew close the door was flung open, and whilst willing hands helped him down his horse was led away by a groom to the stables.

His wet clothes were taken from him, he was given a hot supper, and then he settled down for the night in a warm feather bed. Refreshed and relaxed he was up early next morning, as he knew friends in Stroud would be anxious for his safety. Breakfast was waiting although there was no one about, and when he went out to the stable yard he found his horse saddled and ready. He shouted for the Inn Keeper but no one came, nor could he find any other servants. Impatient to be away he placed two golden coins on the table and set off on his journey.

He had not gone far when he met his friends, out early to search for him, having feared for his safety in the blizzard. Cheerfully he told them of his luck in finding the Inn, but they protested,

"There isn't an Inn for miles around on these hills,"

"But of course there is," he declared. "Come back with me and I'll show you".

Retracing the hoof marks of his horse in the snow he led them back, but there was no Inn to be seen.

"We told you there isn't an Inn up here," they said.

"But there must be – I stayed there," and he dismounted to look more closely, and there at his feet in the snow lay two golden coins, such as he had left on the table just a short while ago.

Did such an event occur? There is no proof, but the story is no stranger than others in this book known to be true, and the legend has persisted for well over one hundred years.

Owlpen Manor

Ghosts are usually expected in old houses, and their presence in OWL-PEN MANOR has been confirmed to me by Nicholas Mander, who with his wife and family have owned the house for the last 20 years. There is documentary history of this lovely house as far back as 1080 so although at roof level the building is early Tudor, the foundations are Saxon. The de Olepennes lived there until 1490 when the house passed by marriage to the Daunt family who occupied it until 1805.

The great hall was built by one of the Daunts and somewhere in it is a large flagstone covering one of several springs which run beneath the house. There is also a well, said to be Holy, which Nicholas Mander and his wife have had relined. Having lovingly cared for the house since they bought it 20 years ago, now that their children have grown up they open it to the public.

The oldest ghost is thought to be that of Queen Margaret of Anjou, who it is alleged slept in the Tapestry Room the night before the Battle of Tewkesbury. It is said to have been her last happy night, because her son was killed the next day on Bloody Meadow at Tewkesbury, she was captured, and the Yorkist Edward IV was made King.

Her ghost, a grey figure, is seen quite often, and although the Manders have not seen her themselves, Karin Mander's father has done so. One visitor who saw the figure spent the rest of the night with the lights on, but young evacuees billeted at the house during the last War were said to have been delighted by the pretty dress worn by the lady they saw on their first night.

In recent years a teenage boy, staying with his family in one of the holiday cottages, also saw her, whilst a woman visitor was awakened by the strong smell of medieval spices.

Because of these events, Karin Mander has hung dried lavender and buttercups around the four poster bed in the Tapestry Room, a Swedish custom said to drive away evil spirits.

At the other end of the house the figure of a monk has been seen. Known as the Black Monk he has been described as a good and holy man, but no one knows why he appears at OWLPEN MANOR. There was also a room in the house which was kept sealed for close on 100 years, and when it was opened at the end of the last century it was found to contain masses of manuscripts and papers. From among them, it is said, out flew many birds, which vanished into dust as they left the confines of the room. The story was published at the time and it was then disclosed that during the long period when the house was owned by the Daunts, one member of the family was reputed to be a wizard and an alchemist. Modern day dowsers visiting the house described the room as having a bad, or negative feeling.

Nowadays, there are many foreign visitors to Owlpen Manor and Nicholas Mander finds their stories interesting. The Japanese, for instance, describe ghosts in their country as always being without legs, whereas visitors from South Korea are fascinated by the age of the house and of the fact that it has been occupied for so many centuries, as there are no ancient buildings in their country.

Why not take the time to visit on an open day? Who knows, you may be lucky enough to see Queen Margaret of Anjou.

The Walk

Route: Uley – Owlpen – Owlpen Farm – Uley.

Distance: 2 miles.

Terrain: Chiefly footpaths over rolling fields. One short steep minor road stretch at Owlpen.

Finding Uley: Uley lies on the B4066, two miles east of Dursley. O.S. Landranger Sheet 162 (Gloucester and Forest of Dean).

Park and Start: As near as possible to the Green, opposite the church. GR 793986

The Route

❑ From the village green, with the Old Crown Inn on the right, follow the waymark on the power pole between houses. The path goes through gardens and then down to a stile.

❑ Cross a field and go over a stream and a stile at the bottom. Follow the yellow waymark half-right over the next field to cross a stiled stone footbridge.

❑ Now turn left over a stile and keeping a stream, and later a lake, on the left, continue over two stiles to reach a road at OWLPEN.

❑ Good views of the MANOR can be had by walking a short way along the footpath opposite. To see the church, turn left along the road and go through the gate indicated on the right.

❑ To resume the walk, retrace the few steps to pass the stile and then continue up the lane. Pass Owlpen Farm on the right.

❑ Just before reaching a left-hand bend, cross a stile on the right (notice the dog gate) to enter a field.

❑ Keep the boundary on the right as far as a stile. Descend the next field to another stile. Now go half left to cross the next stile, beyond which the path proceeds across a paddock via yet another stile.

❑ Continue to the far corner of the next field to reach a gate. Instead of going through, turn right down the field side to a stile at the bottom. From here, cross another field to a stile at the far left-hand corner.

❑ Climb to the right along a grassy path towards Uley, the roofs of which can be seen over the brow of the slope.

❑ Cross a final stile and keep on by gardens to pass the Prema Arts Centre to reach the main road (B4066). Turn right up the village street to the start.

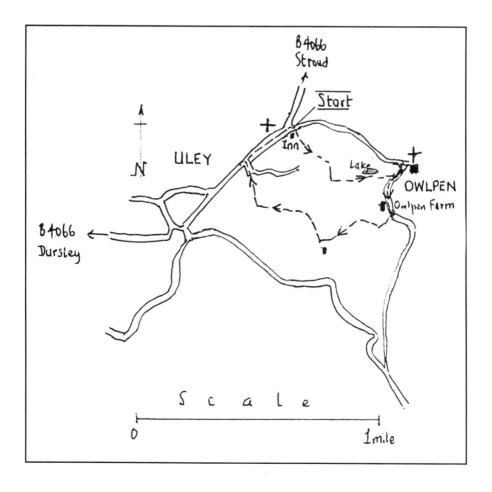

Points of Interest

A large village straggling along the B4066 between Frocester Hill and Dursley, Uley reveals many signs of past prosperity. Its array of elegant houses, varying in style from Tudor to Georgian, reflect its importance in the Cotswold cloth trade. The reputation of 'Uley Blue' as a superior cloth from which military uniforms were made during the 18th and 19th centuries was second to none, standing alongside 'Stroud Scarlet' as synonymous for quality.

This cloth was manufactured in a chain of water mills strung out along the valley of the tiny River Ewelme, the tributary of the river Severn upon which Uley stands. It is said that 30 of these mills were working flat-out during the Napoleonic wars, when, some say, the weavers of Uley supplied not only the British army but the French too!

Although the handsome St. Giles' church was extensively restored during the last century, a few remnants of the original building still survive. One of these, perched high in the tower and therefore difficult to read, is a monument to a 17th century clothier, John Eyles, depicting his personal cloth mark and proclaiming his distinction as the first to make Spanish cloth in Uley.

When, in the 1830s, the Cotswold cloth boom finally ended, out-priced by competition from Yorkshire, the folk of Uley experienced sudden and extreme poverty. The closure of Edward Shepherd's mill in 1837 threw almost a thousand people out of work. Many emigrated to America and Australia, others sought work in the coal-mines of South Wales, while others faced the indignity and privation of the workhouse.

For years, Uley, like its neighbours, knew lean times. Today, however, the village has a quietly prosperous air and its fine Cotswold stone houses, shops and inns suggest a thriving community.

A mere mile distant is the hamlet of Owlpen – manor house, church and a couple of farms. Set against a backdrop of dense woodland, it presents a picture as timelessly beautiful as any to be found in the region.

The Manor House, medieval in origin, has been lovingly restored as a family home after years of neglect. The church, rebuilt in the 1820s and later refurbished in sumptuous Victorian-Edwardian style, is worth the climb to see.

Refreshments

Owlpen Manor, Owlpen, Nr. Uley: Romantic medieval manor house half mile east of Uley, off B4066. Manorial outbuildings; Grist Mill; Formal gardens; Restaurant in Tithe Barn. Open 1st April/30th September – Tuesday, Thursday, Sunday and Bank Holidays – 2 pm/5.30 pm. Patries of 20 or more at other times by appointment. Holiday cottages. Estage Office Tel: 0453 860261.

King's Head Inn, Uley: Traditional Inn.

Nearby Attractions

Uley Bury: Ancient Hill Fort. Admission Free.

Uley Tumulus, (Hetty Pelger's Tump) Off B4066: Chambered Long Barrow. Key obtainable from nearby house. Admission Free.

Coaley Peak, Off B4066: Viewpoint and picnic site.

11

BEVERSTON & CHAVENAGE

CHAVENAGE HOUSE has something to offer every visitor. It is beautiful; it is historic; and its interior is known to thousands of TV viewers because it is a popular venue for today's TV producers.

Scenes were shot there for the House of Elliot and when Grace and Favour was televised the whole cast moved into the house for the filming.

Chavenage has been in the Manor of Horsley since Anglo-Saxon times and, as with so many manors in Gloucestershire, Henry VIII had a hand in its history. After the dissolution he granted the manor to the Seymour family, but in 1564 it came into the possession of Edward Stephens of Eastington who reconstructed and enlarged the house. The initials ES and IS and the date 1576 can still be seen on the porch and the most famous ghost story of the House is connected with his descendant, Colonel Nathaniel Stephens, who lived there during the Civil War.

He was related by marriage to Oliver Cromwell and whilst he was the leader of a body of moderate Parliamentarians, he still had some regard for Charles I.

At the end of the fighting, when Charles I was held in custody, Oliver Cromwell visited Chavenage with Henry Ireton to persuade Nathaniel Stephens to vote for the King's impeachment, but although they argued throughout the night they could not get him to agree.

Not long afterwards, however, they returned again and this time Stephens reluctantly gave in, to the great dismay of his daughter Abigail. She raged at her father, horrified that the family should be associated with the act of regicide and she swore that they would be cursed for evermore.

Whether the curse had anything to do with it or not Colonel Stephens developed a long and painful illness shortly afterwards. As he lay dying friends and neighbours drove to Chavenage to pay their last respects, filling the courtyard with their coaches. Suddenly an exceptionally handsome coach drew up in front of them all, richly caparisoned and drawn by a fine black horse.

As visitors and servants alike watched in amazement they saw the figure of Colonel Stephens, clad in a shroud, glide into the coach. The door was opened and closed by unseen hands and as it drew quickly away the frightened onlookers saw that the headless driver was wearing royal vestments with the Garter on his leg and the Star of the illustrious Order on his breast. As it reached the gateway the coach vanished in flames but, it is said, it is always seen again when the owner of CHAVENAGE dies and it arrives to take him away.

Chavenage House

The two tapestry rooms in the house are the ones in which Cromwell and Ireton slept during their visits over three hundred years ago. When scenes were being shot for the House of Elliot, Jack, one of the leading actors, lay on Cromwell's bed but found it impossible to sleep and had to get up and ask for coffee. On another occasion one of the BBC's electricians complained of feeling hands around his throat in this room and refused to return to it.

At one end of the ballroom there are two doors. One day, when both were open, a member of the family saw a figure pass one, but not the other. He hurried to investigate, but there was no one there. "He rushed from the room, white as a sheet," I was told, declaring, "I've just seen a ghost".

The grandfather of the present owner of CHAVENAGE HOUSE was a Roman Catholic priest and he, as well as an Anglican vicar, exorcised one of the rooms at the request of a member of the family, apparently without success as the room is still said to be haunted.

The son of the present owner slept there during his childhood, but it was not until recent years that he revealed he was afraid there and always slept with a pillow over his face. It is now a spare room and visitors have complained of finding the door locked in the night, although it is always open in the morning.

There are four doors in Colonel Stephens' room, but a visiting member of the family complained when she slept there someone always bumped into the bed, as they might have done if walking across the room from one door to the other. The bed has now been moved and stands in an unusual position in the room, but the occupant is no longer disturbed.

A more gentle story of the house is that during the Civil War a girl living there used to put a candle in the tiny oblong window in the little porch facing the garden to let her lover, at Beverston Castle, know there were no Parliamentarian soldiers about and it was safe for him to keep his tryst. They have left no ghosts, so let's hope they went safely on their way.

There are other ghosts, however, at Chavenage. The CHAPEL is not as old as the house, but the building incorporates much earlier stone work and a monk has been seen there kneeling in prayer, life-like enough for a visitor not to realise he had seen a ghost. Chavenage has always been in the Manor of Horsley so perhaps he was once one of the community of Augustinian Monks who came from Tours to settle at Horsley after the Norman conquest.

Many stirring events have taken place at Chavenage House, leaving their mark in more ways than one, but only one family has owned the property since 1561. There is usually one of them around to welcome visitors and to tell stories which bring the history of Chavenage alive.

The Walk

Route: Beverston – Chavenage Green – Chavenage House – Chavenage Lane – Beverston.

Distance: $3^3/_4$ miles.

Terrain: Flat, easy walking, chiefly along well-used bridleways.

Finding Beverston: The village lies just off the A4135, $1^1/_2$ miles west of Tetbury. O.S. Landranger Sheet 162 (Gloucester and Forest of Dean).

Park and Start: In Beverston, near the church. GR 862940

The Route

❑ With the churchyard wall on the right, walk up to a gateway. Cross a cattle grid and turn right along a field path, keeping a wall on the right.

❑ When the wall ends, keep virtually the same line but with a hedge on the left. Cross a stile by a gate and continue (the hedge having swung away to the left), across a field to join a bridleway at a gate beyond a hollow.

❑ Go through the gate and follow the bridleway – narrow at first, wider later – to pass Chavenage Green Cottages and reach a road through a gateway.

❑ Turn right along the wide verge of an avenue of limes to reach CHAVENAGE HOUSE. After seeing the house, retrace steps as far as a signposted bridleway (now on the left) just beyond ornamental gate pillars. Pass between barns to join a track (Chavenage Lane), which soon narrows and keeps a wall on the left.

❑ The track is less evident beyond two gates. At this point, follow the direction indicated by the blue waymark. This entails climbing the field ahead, then keeping a hedge on the right to pass through a gate at the top of the slope.

❑ From here, a clear track leads towards the A4135.

❑ On reaching this busy road, turn right for 40 yards, then cross to follow another bridleway sign across two fields.

❑ Immediately beyond a gateway with a blue waymark, turn right to follow a track between hedges back to Beverston.

❑ Cross the A4135 once more to reach the church and the start.

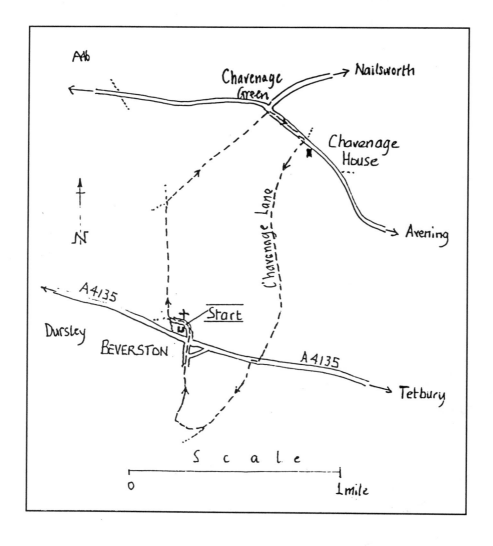

Points of Interest

The south Cotswold scenery on this walk is gentle rather than exciting but even so, the views from the network of wide inviting bridleways make for pleasant walking. The one dominant landmark is the handsome spire of Tetbury church, dwarfing the other buildings of the little town glimpsed through the wayside trees.

Many of these trees, spaced out at regular intervals along the bridleways, are oaks – venerable specimens with vast crowns. A good number of old ashes are passed too, while the short stretch of road walking between Chavenage Green and House is beautified by a splendid avenue of limes.

Beverston, from which the walk commences, is a delightful little village which amply rewards a leisurely exploration. Prominent amongst its engaging cluster of buildings is its castle, one of the few to be found in the Cotswolds and now a romantic ruin. History tells us that a fortified building of some kind stood here in pre-Conquest times, and that Earl Godwin and his kinsman, Harold, made use of it when applying pressure on King Edward the Confessor regarding the succession. A century later, during the 'Nineteen long winters' of the reign of King Stephen, this same building was besieged by none other than Queen Maud, the king's mother.

The present castle dates from the 13th century and originally had four drum towers arranged round a quadrangle. Extra refinements, such as a gate-house, were added later and access was by a drawbridge over an encircling moat.

During the Civil War, Beverston was besieged twice and local legend has it that it fell to the Parliamentary troops because its Royalist commander, Colonel Oglethorpe, was occupied courting a local lady instead of attending to his duties.

Today, Beverston castle is a private residence, open to the public only on limited occasions. Even so, good views of it can be had from the roadway leading to the starting point by the church.

St. Mary's is a Norman church with 13th, 14th and 15th century additions. A comprehensive restoration was carried out in 1844 by Lewis Vulliamy, on instructions from R.S. Holford of Westonbirt, who had bought the estate. Perhaps the most outstanding features are the beautiful 13th century south arcade and the striking weather-beaten sculpture of the Resurrection high on the outer wall of the tower, and said to be Saxon.

Beverston Castle

A buttressed barn opposite the castle is worth inspection, while a venerable old walnut tree close by is also buttressed, but by wooden supports.

Chavenage House is a fine Elizabethan manor house. Some idea of its splendour can be obtained from the road but a visit on one of its opening times is strongly recommended.

Chavenage gained prominence immediately after the Civil War when its owner, the Parliamentarian Colonel Edward Stephens, was visited by Oliver Cromwell, who persuaded him to support the Bill of Impeachment leading to the trial and execution of Charles I.

Nearby, and viewed from the route of the walk, are some distinctive farm buildings, including 17th century barns.

Refreshments

Chavenage House, Chavenage, Tetbury: Historic Elizabethan house. Open Thursdays, Sundays including Easter Sunday and Bank Holidays. May/September – 2 pm/5 pm. Groups can be organised any day throughout the year by appointment. Pre-booked teas and other meals. Admission charge. Tel: 0666 502329.

Westonbirt Arboretum, Nr Tetbury: Visitor Centre and Refreshments. March/December inclusive. Admission charge. Grounds open all year 10 am/8 pm (or dusk if earlier). Tel: 0666 880220.

Hare & Hounds Hotel, Nr. Tetbury: Accommodation and meals.

Choice of hotels, inns and cafes in Tetbury.

Nearby Attractions:

Westonbirt Arboretum: See above.

Police Bygones Museum, 63 Long Street, Tetbury: Open Easter to October – Monday/Saturday – 10.15 am/4.15 pm.

12

NAILSWORTH AND THE AVENING ROAD

The wool and stone of the Cotswolds attracted the Romans so that it became one of the most densely populated regions of Roman Britain and in medieval times the Cotswolds emerged as the world's foremost producers of wool and woollen cloths, but the beauty of the countryside was never destroyed.

The roads leading along the valley from Stroud are thickly lined with trees, but when Nailsworth is reached there is a sense of the industrial past, although it is here that the "super-tramp" W.H. Hudson came in 1931 to finally settle in Glendower, a two-storeyed cottage overlooking the valley, and where no doubt he had time "to stand and stare".

Mills once famous for cloth making now have a reputation as riverside restaurants or craft and cultural development centres but a stroll through some of the winding back streets and alleys can lead to the discovery of curiosities, like Stokescroft in Cossack Square, where Russian prisoners were held during the Crimean War, but for those seeking haunted places a headless horseman has been seen just above Longford's Cloth Mill on the Nailsworth to Avening Road.

No one seems to know why he, and others like him, haunt this road, but it was fairly commonplace at one time to behead an enemy rival. Henry VIII even got rid of his wives in that way and it is said that he is sometimes heard sighing at Windsor, as well he might, but no one ever seems to see or hear the ghost of an executioner.

The stories told to me in Nailsworth, however, are of modern ghosts. When friends bought a house in the Forest Green area they were frequently disturbed by the sound of a child running and crying pitifully, "Mummy, Mummy," but they were never able to discover why, as no one remembered a child at the house. Many ghosts like that one seem to be seen or heard frequently, but Cyril Shackleford sent me this story of a solitary visitation:

"My grandparents," he wrote, "were named Widdup. Grandfather was quiet and level-headed, but delighted to tell people he was descended from the Stansfield Widdups, owners of Stansfield Hall on the Lancashire/Yorkshire borders.

As he grew older he became obsessed with tracing the family tree, and of proving his right to this title. All of his spare time was spent in research, but he was shocked when he discovered his favourite aunt Emily, who had died some years before, was of illegitimate birth. This had been a closely guarded secret throughout her lifetime, and he had never even suspected it.

By the time he retired he had acquired a mass of information, and he devoted his entire spare time to collating it, in the certain knowledge that he could prove his right to be called Lord of the Manor. He told my grandmother though he was sorry this would mean exposing Emily's illegitimacy.

One day, as usual after lunch, he retired to his study to continue his work. Suddenly my grandmother heard him cry out in alarm. She ran into the study, and found him, white as a sheet, gripping the arms of his chair.

"I've just seen Emily," he said. "She's come back because she's upset and doesn't want people to know she was illegitimate. I musn't go on with this work."

He refused to talk about it afterwards. He did not do any more research and he did not complete the family tree. Eventually he burned all the documents, so that the family never knew the whole story."

The Walk

Route: Nailsworth – B4014 – Wood Lane – Shiptons Grave Lane – Hazel Wood – Pensile Road – Nailsworth.

Distance: $2^3/_4$ miles.

Terrain: Chiefly along footpaths, bridleways and minor roads. A few gradients and wet patches, especially around and beyond Hazel Wood.

Finding Nailsworth: The town stands on the A46, four miles south of Stroud. O.S. Landranger Sheet 163 (Gloucester and Forest of Dean).

Park and Start: Main car park, Old Market. GR 850997

The Route

From the car park, go down to the A46 and cross to reach the B4014 (AVENING ROAD). Climb the pavement to the summit of Tabrams Pitch.

❑ Just beyond the junction with Church Street, and opposite a bus stop, turn right along Wood Lane, signposted "To bridleway leading to Shiptons Grave Lane".

❑ Beyond a recreation ground, the lane becomes a rough track which climbs between high banks. After passing through a gateway, follow the bridleway sign straight on between fields. Keep on through woodland (gates at each end) and continue past a derelict barn to reach Shiptons Grave Lane through a gate.

❑ Turn left, but instead of taking the lane, follow a blue waymark through a gate. This straight bridleway keeps a wall on the left before entering Hazel Wood through a gate. Inside, take the left-hand of two tracks (i.e. straight on) and follow it (avoiding wet patches along well-worn diversions) to leave through a metal gate leading into a field.

❑ Follow the stream-side path down to the Avening Road, reached through a gate along the bed of a shallow stream.

❑ Cross the road with great care and turn left down to a bridge opposite the Weigh-bridge Inn. Cross the bridge and continue as far as a right-hand bend in the road.

❑ At this point, leave the road and follow a public footpath sign on the left along the drive of a private house. Go through two gates and enter woodland.

❑ Follow the grassy ride to reach a road through a gate.

❑ Turn left along this tree-lined scenic road, which skirts hilly common land (National Trust) before descending along Pensile Road into NAILS-WORTH.

❑ To return to the start, turn left by a cattle grid and cross the A46 once more. The car park is on the left of the road climbing opposite.

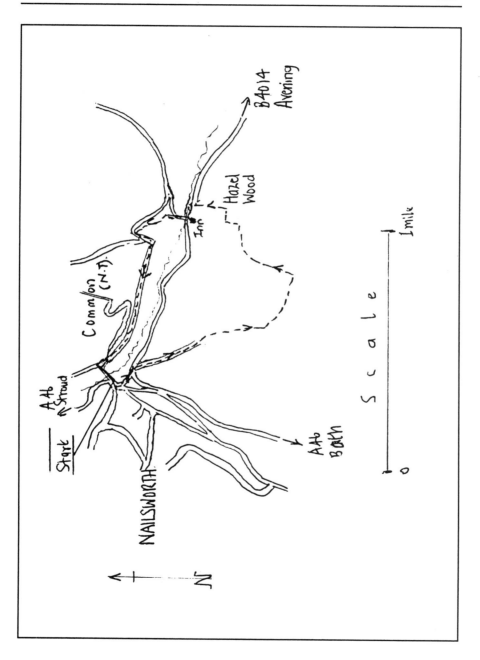

Points of Interest

A little town built at the junction of two valleys, Nailsworth developed as a cloth-making centre and although its mills have long since closed and been converted to other uses, it remains an industrial town in character.

One of these mills, the Dunkirk, is said to have provided the Victorian novelist Dinah Mulock (Mrs. Craik) with the basis for John Halifax's mill in 'John Halifax Gentlemen'; hardly surprising, for although much of the story is set around Tewkesbury, the author lived for some time at nearby Amberley. Nailsworth can boast another notable literary connection. The poet W.H. Davies spent the last years of his life living round about, and his final home, Glendower Cottage at Watledge, remains externally unchanged since his death in 1940.

Modern Nailsworth, astride the busy A46, is a bustling place and the visitor seeking to discover something of its history will soon forsake the traffic- blighted town centre for the tangle of lanes, alleys and footpaths that comprise the heart of the old town.

Worth searching for are the modest weavers' cottages in the valley and the fine houses built by the rich clothiers higher up the slopes. The inns too, have plenty of character, especially the Britannia and the aptly-named Clothiers' Arms, while by contrast, the Friends' Meeting House, off Chestnut Hill, built in 1689, is one of the town's oldest surviving buildings.

The hilly expanse of open country to the east of Nailsworth, along the southern edge of which the concluding stretch of the walk passes, is part of Minchinhampton Common. Covering almost 600 acres, this extensive plateau is second only to Cleeve Common as Gloucestershire's largest expanse of open ground. Now under the care of the National Trust, its unimproved state ensures that its rich variety of lime-loving wild flowers continue to thrive and in their turn encourage the presence in summer of a varied insect population, including several species of butterflies.

Walkers with time and energy to spare may well wish to explore parts of the common on the way back to Nailsworth.

Refreshments

Weighbridge Inn, Longfords, Nailsworth: Popular old Inn; Bar meals.

Egypt Mill, Nailsworth: Restaurant. Tel: Stroud 833449.

Ruskin Mill, Horsley Road, Nailsworth: Coffee Shop. Tel: 0453 62571.

Tubby's Albino's Cottage, George Street, Nailsworth: Breakfasts, lunches, teas, suppers. Handmade chocolates.

Nearby Attractions:

Ruskin Mill, Horsley Road, Nailsworth: Craft workshops and water wheel.

13

RODBOROUGH COMMON

Rodborough Common provides another variation in Gloucestershire scenery, where cattle roam freely from May to October and there are delightful places to walk, but it must have been a wild and lonely spot in the 17th century when Richard Clutterbuck wandered here.

Born into a poor family in 1638 Richard lost his sight at the age of 12, but his remarkable sense of touch and sound became legendary. It is said he could hear when the last grain of sand ran out of an hour glass, or the faintest whisper from another room.

Possessing an inventive mind and skilful hands he constructed various mechanical devices, whilst his love of music led him to make and play violins. He overcame great difficulties and achieved independence and happiness, so perhaps that is why he is not among the rather sad ghosts who haunt this area.

It was also in the 17th century that an Ale House was built, which became The Bear of Rodborough Hotel, taking its name from the bear baiting that took place nearby.

Conveniently located on what was then the main coaching route from Gloucester to London, horses were changed here and it is easy to imagine with what pleasure weary travellers alighted from the coaches to rest and eat.

The welcoming inscription carved above the entrance did not exist in those days, but the words, believed to have been carved by Eric Gill:

"Through this wide opening gate none came too early, none returned too late"

were perhaps appreciated even more by travellers in those days of slow and wearisome journeys. None have stayed to haunt the hotel, but phantom coaches and headless riders gallop along the BEAR – WOODCHESTER ROAD.

Two youths were alarmed by the sight of a coach there one night in 1977 and the event, reported in the Stroud News & Journal, prompted a good deal of correspondence from others who had had similar experiences.

The curator of the local museum suggested that the apparition might be connected with a firm of carriers, Turner & Bayliss who owned the Bear in 1839 and also the house and stables at the Road House known as Rodborough Grange.

A carrying business had been established by Samuel Tanner and continued after his death in 1733 by his son. Eventually a partnership was formed with A.K. Bayliss about 1804 which operated London stage wagons.

A three horse coach operated between STROUD AND BRISTOL soon afterwards, which passed into the hands of John Evans. Known as Sober John, because of his stolid manner and slow movements, it is jokingly thought that he could never have been responsible for the 'FLYING COACHES' which haunt this area. On the other hand, Tanner & Bayliss claimed their 'FLYING WAGONS' which carried cloth, wool and general merchandise, took only as long to travel between Stroud and London as Sober John took to travel to Bristol and back! So maybe their 'flying wagon' is the one still seen around.

The Bear was a frequent call for generations of carriers. Naturally they did not leave without first having a drink, and one driver always relied on his horse to get him home safely. The huddled shape seen sometimes on the road with a phantom vehicle is still believed to be that of the inebriated driver. A Mrs. Hunt, known as "The Bisley God help us Carrier" also called regularly at The Bear to buy a pint, but she gave it to her horse to drink before he began the long pull up to Bisley. They seemed to have settled happily, however, and are not seen among the ghosts on the Common.

In the lengthy correspondence reported in the newspaper in 1977 the ghost of a headless rider was repeatedly mentioned. One man wrote: "It was about five years ago, just after midnight, and I was taking my dog for a walk. Suddenly I saw a horse and a rider who was headless. It was very frightening and the dog was barking."

He said he had no wish to go down 'the haunted lane' again, and this was followed by a letter from a couple who have moved because of their experiences.

Not far from The Bear was a house called RODBOROUGH MANOR which was badly damaged by fire some years ago. In 1971 the STABLES were converted into flats, into which this couple moved, but they left after 15 months because of the eerie atmosphere. They write: "We used to hear horses hooves sounding on the cobblestones, but there were no horses to be seen and the cobblestones had long since gone."

On a summer evening they also saw a stage coach: "We were walking down the same lane and got just below the cattle grid when the stage coach seemed to disappear down the drive leading to the MANOR. It had been raining and we thought it might have been mist, yet we knew it was something more.

We didn't speak about it until we read about it in the paper, and now we know it is true. It definitely had the outline of a stage coach, and it looked as though someone with a tall hat was standing on the back. There was no sound but I cannot remember if there were horses pulling it."

Both husband and wife felt there was an uncanny feeling about the area and their Dalmatian dog "went mad" in the flat, howling, especially at night and scratching at the door, until finally they had to get rid of him.

"Although it was a lovely area to live in," they write, "with those beautiful views down the valley, and the gorgeous countryside all around, we have an awful feeling about the place. I would never walk in the woods and there was an unearthly sort of quiet and no bird song. The atmosphere just got worse and we had to get out. The feeling of evil was unbearable."

It is a pity not to find any pleasant ghosts in the area, but if you feel inclined to prolong your walk by two or three miles and visit the AMBERLEY INN you will find a different king of phantom, of whom no one is afraid.

Sue, a receptionist there for a number of years, told me the staff are all aware of a presence, and frequently see a shadow late in the evenings, sometimes when a group of them are sitting talking together. No one is afraid, but they often experience a chill feeling.

Another receptionist dislikes checking the lounge at night because a figure has been seen there sitting in a chair, but never clearly enough to identify.

The chef, employed at the hotel for the past five years, told me he is always aware of the presence. He has seen a shadow pass an illuminated wine cabinet and has hurried into the Bar to see who is there, but it is always empty. A dog, brought by a visitor, steadfastly refuses to go upstairs.

Sometimes there is mischief abroad. Keys go missing, taps are turned on, and, most puzzling of all, pillows disappear from locked rooms and are never found again.

Occasionally visitors ask to be moved from one particular room, and a male guest there awoke suddenly feeling he was not alone. The second bed showed the indentation of a figure, although there was no one to be seen, and when a woman member of staff slept there she could not move the blankets "because there was someone else in the bed!"

Although no one on the staff is afraid, they would all like the ghost identified. They are inclined to link it with the suicide of a kitchen porter at the hotel some 50 years ago, but have no proof; meanwhile they just wish he would leave the pillows alone.

Rodborough Common - the Bear Hotel and the road down to Rodborough Manor

The Walk

Route: Bear Hotel – Rodborough Common – Bear Hotel.

Distance: $1^3/_4$ miles.

Terrain: Route level throughout, chiefly over open common.

Finding Rodborough Common: Rodborough Common is approximately two miles south of Stroud and can be reached along unclassified roads both from the A46 and A419. O.S. Landranger Sheet 162 (Gloucester and Forest of Dean).

Park and Start: At the southern end of the Common, near the Bear of Rodborough Hotel. GR 854027.

The Route

❑ From the Bear of Rodborough hotel, enter the Common by the clear path to the right of the descending ROAD signposted WOODCHESTER.

❑ The path soon follows a stone wall on the right. At the point where this wall swings sharply away to the right, just beyond a garden fringed with topiary bushes, keep straight on along the path across the Common in the direction of a clump of pines.

❑ On reaching the trees, follow the boundary wall on the left, cross a drive to a house (Braeside) and continue towards the tower of Rodborough Fort, rising prominently ahead.

❑ At a fork in the path before reaching the Fort, go right to strike a roughly-surfaced track at right angles. Turn right along this. Keep right at the next fork and pass to the left of a football pitch.

❑ Cross a private road and continue alongside the Common road past the Hithe. Cross the road by a postbox and follow the clear path towards a crossroads. on reaching this, turn right along the roadside verge.

❑ The Bear of Rodborough Hotel soon comes into view ahead.

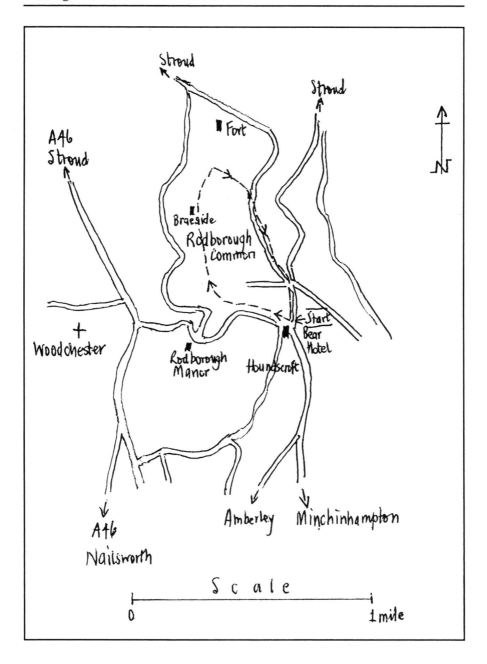

Stroud

Stroud

A46
Stroud

Fort

Braeside

Rodborough
Common

N

Woodchester

Rodborough
Manor

Houndscroft

Start
Bear
Hotel

A46
Nailsworth

Amberley

Minchinhampton

S c a l e

0

1 mile

Points of Interest

Together with its near neighbour, Minchinhampton Common, Rodborough Common comprises an elevated plateau to the south of Stroud. Close-grazed by generations of sheep – and rabbits too – Rodborough Common is now under the care of the National Trust and visitors can roam at will, enjoying fresh air, sweeping vistas and a rare spaciousness beneath open skies.

There is evidence of human activity on this lofty hill top in prehistoric times. Two early Bronze Age spearheads have been excavated, together with finely embossed bronze bands, while other digging has unearthed first century AD pottery and what appeared to be the ditch of an early Roman fort.

Until the late 14th century, Cotswold upland commons such as Rodborough supported extensive beechwoods. Commoners exercised their ancient rights of pasturage, especially of pigs, in these woods but gradually felling and charcoal-burning depleted them and created the open downland we see today.

This limestone grassland forms a valuable wildlife habitat. Rodborough, like other surviving Cotswold commons, is scheduled as a site of special scientific interest (SSSI). Unfortunately however, the demand for grazing has declined in recent years and this had led to the spread of coarse vegetation which threatens to choke the wild flowers. Even so, a remarkable range of limestone flora is present on the Common, including cowslip, rock-rose, salad burnet, milkwort, field scabious and wild thyme. The abundance of these flowers ensures a varied butterfly population, especially of blues, skippers and fritillaries.

For centuries, a road crossed Rodborough Common and it was to serve travellers along this rough upland highway that the Bear Inn was built early in the 17th century. An advertisement dated 1796 states that Daniel Niblett, a carrier, had a warehouse at the inn, from which his London waggon departed every Monday 'precisely at twelve o'clock at noon, and arrives at the George Inn, Snowhill, in London, every Friday morning, and returns to the Bear Inn aforesaid every Thursday'.

On a ledge at the south western limit of Rodborough Common by the Woodchester road stood Rodborough Manor, built in the Italian style by the 18th century prison reformer Sir George Oneisiphorus Paul. This was later the home of Sir John Russell M.P., father of Bertrand Russell, but was burnt down in 1900. Its successor stands surrounded by fine beeches.

The most prominent building on the Common itself is the so-called Rodborough Fort, a folly built in the 1760s by George Hawker, a prosperous dyer. It serves now as the centre of a caravan park.

Although the suggested route is a short one of less than two miles, keen walkers may well wish to extend this by wandering further afield across the Common. While for those content to sit and contemplate the view, there are plenty of well-sited seats to choose from.

Refreshments

The Bear of Rodborough, Nr. Stroud: 17th century (Forte) hotel. Takes its name from bear baiting which used to take place nearby. Accommodation; Restaurant and bar meals. Tel: 0453 878522.

Burleigh Court Hotel, Minchinhampton: 18th century hotel. Accommodation; Meals.

Amberley Inn, Amberley: Cotswold stone Inn. Panoramic views. Accommodation; Lunches. Tel: Stroud 872565

Nearby Attractions

Selsley Herb & Goat Farm, Water Lane, Selsley (off B4066): Open 1st April/30th September – 10 am/5.30 pm. Admission Free.

Minchinhampton Common: Owned by National Trust. Contains ancient earthworks. Open at all times.

14

BOWBRIDGE LANE & NETHER LYPIATT

Stroud, situated at the meeting point of five deep valleys, is an interesting place to visit when time allows. For centuries a centre of the West of England wool trade, it has kept pace with time and today bristles with activity, although like all old towns it has its share of legendary stories.

In St. Lawrence church-yard, for instance, can be found the grave of Joseph Francis Delmont, a 21 year old Lieutenant of His Majesty's 82nd Regiment who is believed to have been the last man slain in a duel in England.

Many writers are to be found in the area, including Laurie Lee, author of the well-loved book *Cider with Rosie*, who lives in the nearby Slad Valley.

As in so many parts of the country there are ghosts in abundance, but the first story, sent to me from STROUD by Mrs. Garvey, seems to be of poltergeist activity:

"I lost my husband in June 1978 after a long illness. I was left with a big mortgage on a large house so I sold as quickly as I could and bought a small one, where I still live.

A door to the cellar leads off the living room. On our second evening here there was a rapping and knocking on the cellar door. My sixteen year old daughter Nicye was with me and we were both very frightened as we thought someone was locked in the cellar.

Eventually when the knocking stopped we opened the door, but there was no one there. Then it started again so I went into the cellar and listened at all the pipes etc. and took down a few things hanging on the door which might have caused noises, but after a short time there came a few more taps. with an occasional loud knock. Just as Nicye was going to bed it began again, a soft rat-tat-tat, so she got up, opened the cellar door and said loudly:

"Are you a ghost? If so I'm sorry if you don't like us, but we won't hurt you!"

I can't remember what else she said, but she talked to the knocking and then said goodnight to it. We went to bed and there was no more knocking that night.

After that Nicye always said, "Hello, what do you want?" and had a chat to the knocking. The trouble was when we were upstairs we could not tell if the knocking was from the cellar, or someone at the front door. Many times I went to the front door expecting to find a visitor, only to realise the knocking had come from the cellar.

One morning Nicye went to work early and four times I got out of bed, thinking someone was at the front door. When Nicye came home I told her I was fed up with her ghost, as when I wanted a lie-in it kept waking me up. Anyway, not long after that came a tap on the cellar door. Nicye went straight over to it and told the ghost off for waking me, and told it not to tap early in the morning again, but to wait for her. Never again did it tap, or knock in the morning.

My son came home to live early in 1980 and wanted to make the cellar into a workshop. I told him that was fine, but that Nicye had a ghost there whom we hadn't seen, only heard. He said it was only old water pipes, or next door and he would soon find out the cause. He never did, but like me he got used to it and to Nicye talking to it. It was quite usual in the middle of tea for the knocking to start and for Nicye to shout "Shut up! I'm having my tea" or "Be quiet now please – I'll talk to you later.'

It only knocked now when Nicye was at home, so we grew accustomed to it, but when visiting grandchildren came they were frightened, so we told them the noises came from next door"

Poltergeist activity often occurs when there are teenagers in the house. This seemed to be the case here for when, tragically, 16 year old Nicye was killed in a road accident in August 1980 her mother continued to live in the house, but the noises were never heard again.

A story of a very different kind was sent to me by Mrs. Griffiths, who wrote:

"I was born at BAY TREE COTTAGE, BOWBRIDGE LANE, near Stroud, and lived there until I was about eight years of age. I was one of 11 children, and although some of them had grown up and left home by the time I was born, there was always a crowd of us around, which was just as well as our cottage was haunted by a ghost we children called Old Grimes.

With such a large family it took some ingenuity to find sleeping space so one of my brothers had a bed on the wide landing at the top of the stairs. From this landing a passage led to the middle room, where mum and dad slept, and also to a large room at the end used by the girls. A door on the landing opened on to stairs leading to the attic.

At that time, more than 40 years ago, we had no electricity and there was no water supply to the cottage. One of my brothers always went out to the pump and brought in a bucketful of water last thing at night, ready for morning. One night, from his bed on the landing, he saw a figure go downstairs, and he thought it was my mother as she always liked a glass of water by her bed. Getting out of bed he hurried downstairs after her and called, "Here's some water Mum.'.

The figure turned round sharply and gave my brother an awful fright – it was an old grey-bearded man, who looked startled, then disappeared through the flagstones!

If we had visitors they had to sleep on the sofa in the front room, leading off the kitchen. One man who slept there was tipped off and the sofa turned upside down. When one of my married brothers came from Worcester with his wife, they had to sleep in the front room. During the night his wife woke him up, saying she was afraid as she could feel something moving above her. My brother had put a candle and matches on a chair, but when he put out his hand he could not feel chair or candle, although they were there next morning.

We girls used to hear footsteps at night, and a sound we thought was Old Grimes' braces dangling. When the noises were very loud we sometimes were afraid, and would call mum and dad, and none of us would ever stop in the house alone. We had a dog too and there were times when his hair would bristle and he would start growling, then we'd know Old Grimes was about again. Although we did not see him, we were always aware that something, or someone was around.

It was not easy to find a cottage to rent which was big enough for our large family, but when I was about eight we moved. The next tenant was very unhappy, however, and refused to pay rent because of the disturbances, and she did not stay long.

According to local history two elderly brothers had lived in the cottage for years, but eventually one was suffocated by the other. One of them, I think, must have been Old Grimes."

It was on the STROUD/BISLEY road where the next ghost was seen as Mr. Liddicott of Bisley wrote to tell me:

"During the years 1918 to 1925 my father used to cycle from Stroud to Bisley on Saturday nights to get the Sunday joint, because the butcher sold meat cheaply when it got late as he did not have a cold store.

One night, on his way home, my father could see someone pushing a bike, with a light on it, near the top of STROUD HILL. He thought he would hurry and catch him up for company on the ride home, but no matter how he hurried the man seemed to stay the same distance ahead.

Reaching the top of the hill my father got back on his bike, and so did the person in front, both riding towards Lypiatt Lodge. In those days there was a very high nut hedge on the left-hand side of the road, and suddenly my father saw the light on the other bike go right over the top of the hedge. He rode as hard as he could to the spot, expecting to find the other man injured, but there was no trace of him or of this bike!

My father was very shaken but he didn't say anything to anyone for a while because he thought he'd be accused of "seeing things". However my grandfather was landlord of the George Inn at Bisley at that time, and a few weeks later a man went into the pub, looking very uneasy, and described seeing exactly the same thing."

Nether Lypiatt Manor

It is unlikely we shall ever know the explanation of that story, and although Gloucestershire is popular with ghosts, it also seems attractive to members of the royal family. Prince and Princess Michael of Kent bought NETHER LYPIATT MANOR, a beautiful Queen Anne house, a few year's ago.

Situated on Lypiatt ridge the house occupies a prominent position and is popularly known as "the haunted house".

It was once owned by Judge Charles Cox, born in 1661. Educated at St. Edmund Hall, Oxford, he became a barrister and had a distinguished career. He was also M.P. for Cirencester for a number of years, as well as for Gloucester.

His wife, Catherine Chamberlayne, brought him Nether Lypiatt Manor which he rebuilt in 1717. Ever since his death in 1722 there has been a story that he tried and condemned a smith for murder, but reprieved him so that he could make the ornate ironwork gates in the forecourt of the house. When the work was completed, however, the smith was hanged, and his ghost is said to haunt the site, but the story is disputed by many who consider it out of character for Judge Cox.

There is also a story that prior to the Siege of Gloucester King Charles made the Manor his headquarters and the gates are said to open on the 28th January in honour of his martyrdom. True or not, legends of hauntings persist.

In March 1993 the Gloucestershire Echo published a feature story about Princess Michael when she is alleged to have said "We thought at first that the asking price (for the house) was too high in proportion to the amount of work required . . . we were eventually successful in buying it when foolish stories concerning a ghost appeared in the media and seemed to discourage the bidders."

Foolish stories they may be but a few years before she and the Prince purchased the house a Gloucestershire vicar was called there and said of his visit, "I did not perform an exorcism but I recommended certain things." More recently two other clergymen have been called to the house and gave it a blessing. Meanwhile the locals still call it The Haunted House.

The Walk

Route: Bowbridge Lane – Coneygre Wood – Nether Lypiatt Manor – Claypits Lane – Bowbridge Lane.

Distance: 3 miles.

Terrain: Undulating route along minor roads and public footpaths. Wet patches after rain.

Finding Bowbridge Lane: Bowbridge Lane lies off the A419, three-quarters of a mile south of Stroud. O.S. Landranger Sheet 162 (Gloucester and Forest of Dean).

Park and Start: Bowbridge Lane, reached from Stroud by turning left off the A419 opposite the British Oak Inn. Park on wide stretch of lane near Spider Lane junction. GR 859046.

The Route

❏ Leave BOWBRIDGE LANE along Spider Lane, climbing to the right. On reaching the Crown and Sceptre Inn, turn right along a lane. Pass a cemetery and continue as far as Horns Farm on the right of the lane.

❏ At this point, leave the lane by following a public footpath on the left which climbs into Coneygre Wood. Pass a disused quarry on the left and after crossing a stile, keep a wall on the left.

❏ The path eventually leaves the wood and follows a bank to cross another stile. Climb to cross a further stile and then go over a stream to cross a stile in a fence. At this point, follow the yellow waymark to the right, climbing a steep bank and following a fence on the right. Cross stepping stones, go over a stile, and pass through a handgate (or over a stile alongside). Continue in the direction indicated by the yellow arrow, climbing to go through a gate and along a drive. This leads to a track which in turn leads to a minor road.

❏ Turn right along the road and continue as far as the junction with Claypits Lane on the right, near NETHER LYPIATT MANOR. After viewing the MANOR, turn left along Claypits Lane and follow it as far as the second public footpath sign on the right, indicating Snakeshole and BOW-BRIDGE. This right-of-way follows a lane which after crossing a spring, continues as a descending woodland track. At a fork, keep right and on reaching a junction of several paths, take the left-hand one, (i.e. straight on). Cross a stile and descend to go through a kissing gate.

❑ Continue on the same line down a large field to cross a footbridge. Climb with a hedge on the left, to go through another kissing gate by a cottage.

❑ Continue along a drive to reach BOWBRIDGE LANE and the start.

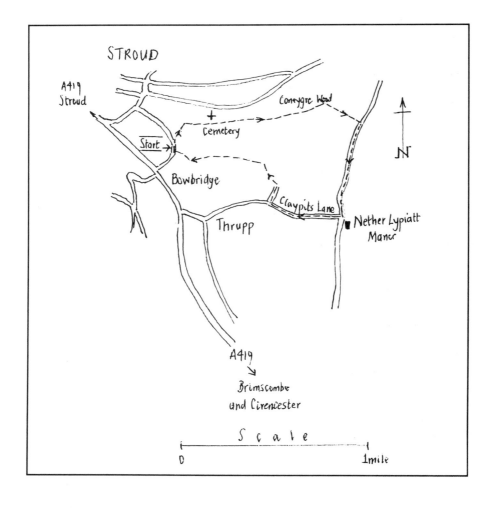

Points of Interest

Although the town of Stroud has a bustling, workaday air, with housing estates reaching out to claim both the surrounding hills and valleys, it is still possible to discover bracing walking country close by.

One such tract of unspoilt Cotswold landscape lies within easy reach to the south-east of the town and can be explored from Bowbridge Lane, off the A419 Frome Valley road. From the top of this lane, the clutter of the town is soon exchanged for pleasant walking, with good views and a rich variety of wild life.

Especially interesting is Coneygre Wood, through which the route passes soon after leaving Bowbridge Lane. Its name, variations of which occur throughout the country, implies it was formerly a rabbit warren. Primarily a beechwood, it has a rich variety of lime-loving spring flowering plants, including dog's mercury, wood anemone, wood sorrel and sanicle, as well as providing breeding habitat for such tree-feeding birds as great, blue and coal tit, nuthatch, treecreeper and great-spotted woodpecker.

Near the entrance to the wood can be seen a disused stone quarry, its working face fully exposed and showing how the beds of oolitic lime-stone were laid down in distant geological time.

Beyond the wood, the route climbs steadily to reach an unclassified road linking the Frome Valley at Brimscombe with Bisley. The name Lypiatt meaning a gate in a woodland fence to confine animals but over which deer can leap, occurs frequently in this area. Lypiatt Park, notorious as the place at which the Gunpowder Plot was hatched, lies to the north-east. The Tudor house of Middle Lypiatt stands almost oppo-site the point at which the road is reached. Nether Lypiatt Manor, a short distance to the south, can be viewed from the public road just alongside the route.

Now the home of Prince and Princess Michael of Kent, Nether Lypiatt is a small yet beautifully proportioned manor house, dating from 1705. It was built for a judge by the name of Coxe and eventually became the property of a noted musician, Mrs. Violet Gordon Wood-house, who, according to the writer Sacheverell Sitwell, 'with her genius brought the music of the past alive'.

Of the house, which he visited often, Sitwell wrote: "No house could compose so beautifully for a glass transparency as Nether Lypiatt, with wrought-iron gates in front flanked by a pair of little formal pavilions or gazebos, and with an interior where music will for ever linger."

Refreshments

Imperial Hotel, Station Road, Stroud: Originally a Coaching and Railway Inn. Accommodation; Meals. Tel: 0453 764077

London Hotel, London Road, Stroud: Accommodation; Restaurant. Tel: 0453 759992

Numerous cafes in Stroud

Nearby Attractions

Stroud District Museum, Lansdown, Stroud: Geology and History. Open weekdays 10.30 am/1 pm; 2 pm/5 pm. Closed Sunday and Bank Holidays.

Lypiatt Hill Farm, Bisley Road, Stroud: Working farm open to visitors. Monday to Saturday 9 am/5 pm. Closed Bank Holiday Mondays. Tel: 0453 764918

15

PAINSWICK

It would be difficult to find any village in the Cotswolds which does not have its own particular beauty, but the people of Painswick claim that those who have not seen their village have not seen the Cotswolds.

Certainly it has an idyllic setting on a hillside, and in full view of the main street is the lovely St. Mary's church, its slender spire rising high from the 15th century tower. Legends abound about the ninety-nine yew trees in the churchyard and table tombs, made by craftsmen, are carefully tended. There is a lychgate and leaflets describing Tomb Trails can be obtained at the church. Cotswold stone houses line winding streets, some of which run steeply down the hillside, providing spectacular views of the countryside.

It is not surprising that many people have moved here when they retired, but there are also old families to be found and traditional ceremonies continue, such as the Clipping ceremony which takes place each year on the Sunday nearest September 19th. It has nothing to do with clipping the yews. 'Clipping' means embracing, which is what the children do as they join hands and encircle the church, singing the Clipping hymn after a short service.

The village is crowded that week as children and grandchildren return home and many say, "Oh I wouldn't miss the clipping". It probably has pagan origins but it evokes a wonderful community spirit. The first time I attended the vicar held up a ten pound note, sent by a publican, who wrote, "It's not often I go to church but I'm always homesick for Painswick on Clipping Sunday".

Puppy-dog pies used to be eaten, plum pies with a small china dog in each. Few now make them but the small china dogs are still to be found in some Painswick homes.

In a place so old ghost stories are to be expected, and at nearby DAMSELLS MILL a phantom coach and horses are seen. Among my collection of tales is a letter sent to me by a lady still living in Painswick, which reads: "I was born and bred in Painswick, like my father and his father before him. It's a lovely place to live, and I suppose my family has always felt "in-tune" with it.

It was my father's habit to walk to DAMSELLS MILL, near the Royal William, to have a smoke each evening. While standing quietly there he told me he frequently saw a coach and horses galloping across the field, in the distance. Whenever it appeared the other horses in the field used to gallop away".

Sightings of coaches are not uncommon in this part of Gloucestershire, and stories abound of black dogs, galloping horses and of animals being granted the gift of speech at Christmas. There is a legendary black dog at nearby Birdlip, but the reason why has been lost in time, unlike a Civil War story in PAINSWICK.

When King Charles I raised his standard at Nottingham in August 1642 he started a war that was to last for several years. Most people have heard of the famous battles like Edge Hill, and of the Siege of Gloucester, but it is not always realised that there were many minor confrontations as well. For instance, between November 1643 and April 1644 there was fighting in 13 places in Gloucestershire, in some places more than once. While Gloucester city, which had declared for Parliament, lay under siege, there were continual skirmishes in the surrounding countryside. Tales are still told of little known events in small towns and villages, like Painswick which had declared for the King. In March 1644 the Parliamentarians were in control there, until Sir William Vavasour, fighting for the King "entered the town with as gallant horse and foot as the King's Army did yield".

His opponent, the Parliamentarian Colonel Massey, placed a guard under a lieutenant, but although he fought with the help of people of the neighbourhood he was eventually forced to take refuge in the church with his men.

The Royalist soldiers are reputed to have hurled hand grenades through the windows, opened up with cannons, and with blazing torches set fire to the church. Soon the whole north aisle was alight, and the large Purbeck marble tomb of Sir William Kington was partially destroyed. On the tower, east and west church walls, marks made by cannon and musket fire are still to be seen. During alterations to the church in 1890/91 a piece of moulding, which had evidently formed part of the doorway at one time, was found buried near the south door. It bore unmistakeable traces of fire.

The men in the church were forced to surrender but the battle was not over for some time. Eventually, however, the town was cleared in the name of King Charles I, but his cause was waning by then and he was beheaded in 1649.

Nights of violence and death are not easily forgotten so tales are still told and vivid stories, not to be found in the records, fill in the details of how it all began. One such story persists concerning the FIERY BEACON GALLERY, a house to be seen in the main street, facing the churchyard.

The Fiery Beacon Gallery as it normally appears

The frontage of this house was extended forward sometime in the late 18th century. Before then, the front door opened on to what was then the village green. It was on this spot, according to the PAINSWICK legend, that the Royalist soldiers gathered to light their torches before storming the church. There was no proof of this, but from time to time rumours arose that a strange light had been seen in the house, and that one room was always icy cold. Just an old wives' tale thought the sceptics.

In August 1984, however, a Canadian and his son-in-law, on a walking tour of the Cotswolds, paused to take photographs in Painswick. They did not have them developed until they returned to Canada, and then were puzzled by one of the Fiery Beacon Gallery because, near the front door, there seemed to be a flame burning on the outside wall, so they wrote to the owners, Mr. and Mrs. Ward at that time:

"We don't remember seeing anything like the flaming image seen on the right-hand side of the building. Would you please be kind enough to let us know if there is anything resembling the flame as seen in the print".

There is no flaming image on that stone wall, so Mrs. Ward replied, telling of the legend, and asking if she could have the transparency. It came with another letter:

"We were very interested to hear of the sensation the picture has caused in your village. I have enclosed the slide from which the print was made. The film I used was ASA 100 Daylight Ektachrome, and as the No. 1 indicates, it was at the beginning of the roll. The film was purchased in Toronto just prior to our trip.

The weather at the time I took the picture, around midday, was overcast. I did not use a flash as it was not needed. The camera used was a 35mm Minox 35GT (made in Germany) and purchased August 2nd 1984."

The slide was carefully examined in England and assurance given that it showed no sign of having been tampered with. Yet the flaming orange torch is there in the picture for all to see, as are the marks of the fire still to be found inside the church.

The Walk

Route: Car park – Churchyard – St Mary's Street – Vicarage Street – Damsells Mill – Paradise – Golf Course – Gloucester Street – Car park.

Distance: $3^3/_4$ miles.

Terrain: Pavements, bridleways and footpaths. Some steep stretches rewarded by fine views.

Finding Painswick: Painswick is on the A46, three miles north of Stroud. O.S. Landranger Sheet 162 (Gloucester and Forest of Dean).

Park and Start: Stamages Lane free car park, off A46. GR 866096.

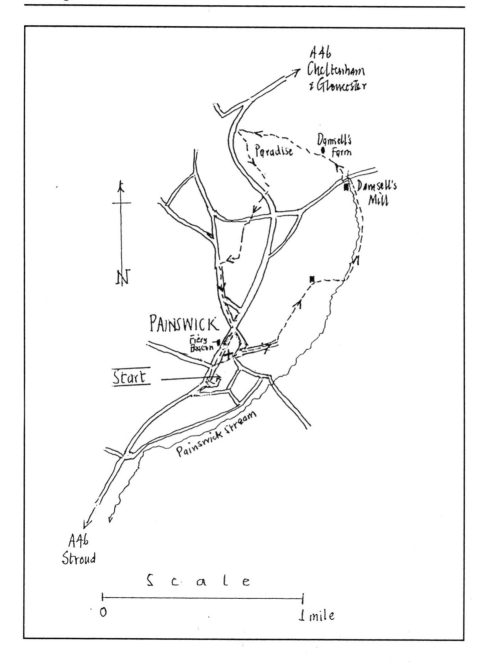

A46
Cheltenham
& Gloucester

Paradise

Damsell's
Farm

Damsell's
Mill

PAINSWICK

Fiery
Beacon

Start

Painswick Stream

A46
Stroud

N

S c a l e

0   1 mile

The Route

❑ From Stamages Lane car park, walk up the A46 and enter the CHURCH-YARD through the Lychgate. On leaving into St. Mary's Street, notice the spectacle stocks alongside the churchyard wall.

❑ Turn left along the street and keep straight on as far as a T-junction.

❑ Turn right here by a former chapel and go down Vicarage Street.

❑ Pass a turn on the right signposted Sheepscombe and continue as far as a public footpath/bridleway sign on the right alongside Museum Cottage.

❑ Follow the bridleway (track) over two cattle grids, through a gate and over another cattle grid. Pass a house on the left, cross a stile, and go through two gates to enter a field.

❑ Keep a fence on the right and after crossing the Painswick Stream, turn left along it just before a gate.

❑ The clear path crosses a stile and passes through a delightful glade. Leave this by another stile to reach a road at DAMSELLS MILL.

❑ Turn left, then right up the lane to Damsells Farm (public footpath). At the point where the lane swings to the right to reach the farmhouse, continue straight on to cross a stile in a hedge.

❑ Follow the yellow arrow over a field to cross a barn enclosure over two stiles. In the next field, veer left to cross a stile alongside a gate.

❑ Beyond, climb half right to enter woodland over a stile.

❑ Another stile gives access to a woodland track. Turn left along this and leave by a gate.

❑ The path now crosses an irregular field half right (beware of wet patches after rain), before climbing to a stile.

❑ A stiffer climb follows up one last field to reach a lane over a stile.

❑ Turn left down into Paradise and continue to reach the A46. Cross with care and follow the footpath sign through a gap in the hedge opposite.

❏ The route crosses a golf green and a golf-club road and keeps straight on over another green to rejoin the road by the drive of a house.

❏ Follow this road all the way to a T-junction. Turn left here, following the Cotswold Way signs into Painswick via Gloucester Street.

❏ On reaching the A46 (New Street) turn right back to the car park, passing the FIERY BEACON GALLERY on the right, opposite the church.

Points of Interest

Well-named "Queen of the Cotswolds" Painswick is a large village of exceptional beauty. Its history can be traced back to Celtic times, when a camp was established on the high ground of Painswick Beacon, to the north of the present village.

It was the quarries of the Beacon area that centuries later yielded the distinctive grey limestone that is the hallmark of Painswick's noble buildings. Although some of these buildings are medieval in origin, most date from the 17th and 18th centuries, when prosperity from the cloth trade was at its peak. Dominating Painswick is the spire of St Mary's church. Dating from the 14th century, this church has a churchyard of exceptional interest. Here can be seen a magnificent collection of 17th and 18th century table tombs, the work of the Bryan family, local masons. Equally famous are the ninety-nine yew trees planted in 1792 and maintained in immaculate condition. Legend has it that any attempt to increase the number of yews to a hundred is doomed to failure.

On St. Mary's Street, alongside the churchyard wall, are the so called spectacle stocks, believed to be the only example of this design to have survived in this country. They date from the 17th century and were last used about 1840.

Painswick's narrow thoroughfares – St. Mary's Street, Bisley Street, New Street, Gloucester Street, Friday Street – all have their share of elegant buildings, some of which are tucked away down even narrower winding lanes. Particularly worth seeking out are the Court House, Castle Hale, Loveday's House, Yew Tree House, Dover House (both passed on the walk), and the Little Fleece, now a National Trust bookshop, not forgetting the Fiery Beacon.

The post office is Painswick's only externally timber-framed building. 18th century Painswick House, with its celebrated Rococo Garden is open to the public.

Spectacle Stocks, Painswick

Damsells Mill dates from 1674. Now a private house, it has at various times served as a cloth mill and a corn mill.

Legend tells us that the hamlet of Paradise is so-named because Charles I described the sheltered combe as such when he took refuge there after the siege of Gloucester. Paradise House is an 18th century mixture of stone and brick, with attractive out-buildings.

Refreshments

Falcon Hotel, opposite Church: 16th century hotel. Accommodation; Restaurant; Bar meals; Bowling Green. Tel: 0452 812189.

Painswick Hotel, Kemps Lane: Palladian – former rectory. Accommodation; Restaurant; Light lunches; Croquet lawn. Tel: 0452 812160.

Several historic inns offer bar meals.

Nearby Attractions

Painswick House, The Stables: Rococo Gardens, open February/mid-December – Wednesday/Sunday including Bank Holidays – 11 am/5 pm. Admission charge.

Church Yard: Famous for yew trees and tomb stones. Leaflets for Tomb Trails available in Church porch.

Guild of Gloucestershire Craftsmen: Hold annual exhibition for month of August.

Prinknash Abbey, Bird Park and Pottery, Cranham, Painswick: Shop selling pottery; Teas. Open daily 9.30 am/ 5 pm. Closed Christmas Day.

16

HAZLETON & PUESDOWN INN

The PUESDOWN INN is only set back a little from the A40 which is a fairly busy road, and yet it still has an air of mystery around it, especially if you pass by on a dark winter's night. Having heard vague stories about a ghost there I went to see the licensee, Mrs. Osborne, a few years ago.

She looked at me suspiciously at first. "I'll only tell you if you believe in ghosts," she said, as apparently the last people to ask had later written jokingly about her story. Once convinced that mine was a serious question, however, she poured out her experiences.

Puesdown Inn

"My husband and I took over this Inn, THE PUESDOWN, fifteen years ago," she began. "It dates from 1236 A.D. and being on the London Road it was a coaching inn at one time. That was about all we knew of its history when we first moved here. Almost before we were settled my parents came to visit us on October 1st 1969, and I put them into the double room, just to the left of the top of the stairs. Next morning they wanted to know what in the world Stan, my husband, had been doing in the night, as they'd been disturbed by his knocking.

He hadn't done any knocking and we couldn't make out what they'd heard. Then my brother came to stay, and he complained about knocking as well. I was so puzzled I suggested we should go out and see if a branch of a tree was blowing against the wall but my brother said it wasn't anything like that; it was rhythmic and loud, knock-knock-knock, pause, then repeat and pause and repeat again. We couldn't make head or tail of it. Then other things happened. My husband was in the bar one day when he felt someone pass him, and he thought it was me, but when he called he found I wasn't in. We both heard footsteps as well; they'd go across the bar and up the stairs. Glasses would tinkle and I sometimes heard the sound of men's voices, talking in strong Gloucestershire accents.

One night eight local men were in the bar. From where I was working I could hear them laughing and talking as they played cards. Then suddenly they stopped; there was complete silence. Going into the bar I asked:

"What's the matter? What's made you so quiet?"

They all looked very startled. They said the front door had opened and closed, footsteps crossed the bar, the counter flap lifted, and the door beyond leading to the stairs had opened and closed... but there was no one to be seen. They'd all watched it happen!

One day I thought I heard my daughter in the bar. She was supposed to be taking her little girl to school, so I called, "Couldn't you start the car love?" She didn't answer, so I went to see what was happening, but there was no one there.

The locals told us the pub had always been haunted. They said in the 18th century a highwayman, known as The Duke, worked this stretch of the old London Road, called The Greenway, and he used to put up here. One night, as he was galloping along, he was shot by a gamekeeper. Somehow he managed to reach the Puesdown. Hammering on the front door he roused the landlord who helped him into the little room we call the lounge, but it was a mortal wound and the Duke died.

It was all very well to know his story, but I got quite nervous when I was alone. One day when I heard his heavy footsteps coming down, I went to the bottom of the stairs, I was so worked up, and I cried out to him:

"Look here you B..... I've got a living to earn. I don't mind you coming in the winter, but you leave me alone when I'm busy in the summer" – and ever since then he's only come from October to February!

I've got used to him now though, as I know he isn't going to do me any harm. A funny thing, though, often when I get to the top of the stairs and turn to go along the corridor, past the little room on my left, I find I've paused as if to let someone go by. And I think to myself, now why did I do that?

And the little room, (next to the double one where my parents were when they heard the knocking), is the one where the Duke used to sleep.

Whenever he comes knocking now I open all the doors and say, "Come in and welcome," but he doesn't come as often as he used to, so I hope the poor soul's at rest!"

The Walk

Route: Hazleton – Lower Barn Farm – Turkdean – Lower Dean – Castle Barn Farm – Old Road – Puesdown Inn – Hazleton.

Distance: $5^1/_2$ miles.

Terrain: Minor roads, bridleways and footpaths, stretches of which may be muddy after rain. A few gentle gradients.

Finding Hazleton: Hazleton lies three-quarters of a mile north of the A40, three miles North West of Northleach. O.S. Landranger Sheet 163 (Cheltenham and Cirencester).

Park and Start: Hazleton village. Near junction of roads signposted Cheltenham, Lower Dean and St. Andrew's Church. GR 079179.

The Route

❑ Walk in the direction of Lower Dean. On reaching a fork, go left along a road indicated as unsuitable for motors. This road extends as far as Lower Barn Farm, beyond which the route proceeds as a track.

❑ Follow this track through two gates. After the second, turn right at a T-junction of tracks and follow a stream along a winding valley.

❑ The track climbs eventually to reach a gate. There is a choice of two alternatives here:

1. Longer route to include Turkdean: Continue through the gate and climb past farm buildings to reach a road. Turn right into Turkdean. Pass the church on the left and continue past a spring, with trough, on the right. Just beyond, turn right down a footpath through trees. At the foot of the slope continue to meet a road.

2. Shorter route omitting Turkdean: Instead of passing through the gate, go through another immediately to the right. Follow the yellow waymark diagonally down a field to pass through a gateway and over a stream to reach a track. Turn right to meet a road.

❑ This is Lower Dean. Turn right along the road. It climbs steadily as far as Castle Barn Farm before levelling out and meeting a road on the right signposted Hazleton, just before the A40.

❑ Follow this road until it bends sharply to the right. Keep straight on here along the OLD ROAD – now a BRIDLEWAY – for about $1^1/_4$ miles to its junction with the A40 just before the PUESDOWN INN.

❑ Walk along the verge past the INN. Cross the car park near the far wall, go through a gate and across a garden to a stile in the far left-hand corner, leading into a field.

❑ Follow the wall on the left to reach a bridleway at a T-junction. Turn left along it and continue to meet a road at Hazleton. Turn right back to the start.

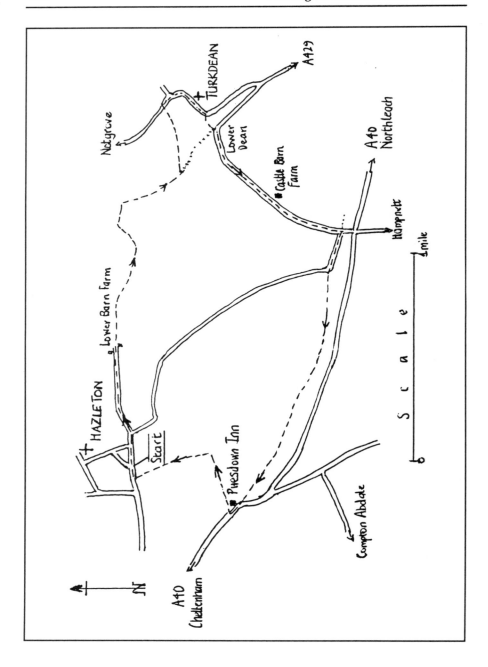

Points of Interest

This is a longer than average walk through rolling wold country as open and remote as any to be found in the north Cotswolds. Hazleton and its near neighbour, Turkdean, typify the small stone-built villages scattered across this spacious landscape, a landscape once given over to the vast sheepwalks of prosperous abbey estates, but now consisting of mile upon mile of walled fields planted with cereal crops.

Both Hazleton and Turkdean possess Norman churches and a good number of traditional Cotswold cottages, farmhouses and handsome barns. A priory of Cistercian monks was founded at Hazleton in the 12th century, as the name Priory Farm, alongside which the walk commences, indicates. It seems likely that the inadequate water supply caused this to be abandoned, however, and the stone used in the construction of the two elaborately carved doorways nearby may well be all that remains of this long-forgotten venture.

Plantings of beech trees are a prominent feature of this landscape. Such a planting separates a stretch of the present A40, built in the 1980s to by-pass Northleach, from the old road, now an overgrown bridleway, along which the route approaches the Puesdown Inn.

In the early years of the coaching era, travellers used this route eastwards rather then risk getting bogged down in the low-lying Leach Valley. Until comparatively recent times, the Puesdown was the only inn on this lonely stretch of ridge road, and it must have been with considerable relief that weary coach passengers alighted here to enjoy the hospitality of this solitary wayside hostelry.

Refreshments

Puesdown Inn, Compton Abdale: Traditional coaching Inn and stopping place for travellers on A40. Bar meals.

Country Hotels: Several interesting and historic hotels and inns face The Square in Northleach (2 miles) offering accommodation and food.

Nearby Attractions

Medieval Church, Northleach: Considered to be one of the noblest in England.

Cotswold Countryside Collection, Northleach: Museum and former House of Correction. Open April/October daily and Sunday afternoons. Admission charge. Tel: 0451 860715.

Keith Harding's World of Mechanical Music, High Street, Northleach: Museum of Antique Clocks, Musical Boxes etc. Open daily 10 am/6 pm. Admission charge. Tel 0451 60181.

17

CHELTENHAM

Cheltenham is often described as the Gateway to the Cotswolds. Known for elegant Regency buildings, public parks and floral gardens, and situated on the edge of beautiful countryside, the town has been famous since the discovery in 1716 of the Cheltenham waters. It has a much longer history than that, however, and tucked away, not far from the tree-lined Promenade, is the medieval Parish church of St. Mary's, famous for its lovely Rose Window.

There are many interesting routes for walks in the town, but for this one it was decided to focus on Pittville Pump Room (where those brave enough can still take the waters), and the Park around it, at the same time pointing the direction to the home of the famous Cheltenham Ghost.

The activities of this ghost in the late 19th century, when the house then called GARDEN REACH belonged to the Despard family, were meticulously recorded by Rosina Despard.

The story has been written so often, and sometimes disputed, that it would not have been included in this book but for a letter I received in September 1982 from Mr. E.S. Lysacht who had known the youngest member of the Despard family. The house, now known as ST. ANNE'S stands in its own grounds in tree-lined Pittville Circus Road, not far from the junction with All Saints' Road. Built around 1860 it was the home for some years of Mr. Henry Swinhoe and his family. During that time Mrs. Swinhoe died and the husband, who had been devoted to her, is alleged to have taken to drink. Within two years, however, he married a woman named Imogen, but the marriage was unhappy.

The children disliked their stepmother and she quarrelled with her husband over his first wife's jewels which he was determined to keep for his children. To make sure of this he instructed a local carpenter to construct a cavity under the morning-room floor, where they were deposited, the boards nailed down and the carpet replaced.

In 1876 Henry Swinhoe died but Imogen had already left him, although she too died two years later at the age of 41. After that an elderly couple lived in the house for a short period, then it was unoccupied for about four years. It was obviously not easy to let even at a low rental, and it was not until 1882 that Captain Despard moved in with his wife, four unmarried daughters, aged 19, 18, 15 and 13 and two sons of 16 and 6. A married daughter who lived away from home visited the family from time to time.

The family had only been living at GARDEN REACH for a few months when Rosina, the 19 year old daughter, first saw the ghost, and Willy, the youngest child, also began seeing it. Fortunately Rosina kept a journal which she sent regularly to a friend in the north of England, and frequent references are made to it in the Morton Papers, written in 1892, by Rosina under the name or R.C. Morton, and held by the Society of Psychical Research.

This is what she wrote of her first encounter with the ghost:

"I had gone to my room but was not yet in bed when I heard someone at the door and went to it, thinking it might be my mother. On opening the door I saw no one, but on going a few steps along the passage I saw the figure of a tall lady dressed in black standing at the head of the stairs. After a few moments she descended. I followed for a short distance, curious as to what it could be. I had only a small piece of candle and it suddenly burnt itself out. Being unable to see more I went back to my room. The figure was that of a tall lady dressed in black of a soft woollen material, judging by the slight sound in moving. The face was hidden in a handkerchief, held in the right hand. This is all I noticed then. But on further occasions I was able to observe her more closely and saw the other side of the left part of the forehead and a little of the hair above. Her left hand was nearly hidden by her sleeve in a fold of her dress. As she held it down a portion of a widow's cuff was visible on both wrists, so the whole impression was that of a lady in widow's weeds. There was no cap on the head, but a general effect of blackness suggest a bonnet and long veil and a hood."

Rosina saw the figure on numerous occasions between 1882 and 1884, often in the drawing room and travelling along the passage to the garden room, where it always disappeared. In the Morton Papers she wrote:

"On or about December 18th 1883 it was seen in the drawing room by my brother and another little boy. They were playing outside on the terrace when they saw the figure in the drawing room close to the window, and ran in to see who it could be that was crying so bitterly. They found no one in the drawing room, and the parlour maid told them no one had come into the house."

Another time, Willey saw the back of the figure going along the passage. When he had first seen her he thought she was real, but once when he and his friends joined hands and made a ring about her, she seemed to walk out between them and disappeared. When the married sister was at home one evening she descended the staircase and saw a figure in black cross the hall into the drawing room. She asked the family, "Who is the Sister of Mercy I've just seen going into the drawing room?" No one knew and a maid was sent to investigate, but there was no one there. Another maid reported seeing a stranger in black entering the house one evening, but again no one could be found.

Rosina's sister Edith was seated at the piano one day when she realised the figure was behind her. She called Rosina who, seeing the ghost standing in the bow window, spoke to it several times, but did not get a reply.

In the Morton Papers she described her efforts to communicate with the ghost. Once she thought it was going to reply, but all she heard was a sort of gasp.

When she placed strings across the ghost's path it simply passed right through them, yet the figure was so solid it was frequently mistaken for a real person. When Rosina tried to touch it she failed and wrote, "It was not that there was nothing to touch, she always seemed to be beyond me, and if followed into a corner simply disappeared."

Footsteps were often heard but, unlike anyone's in the house, they were 'soft and rather slow, though decided and even.'

At times the house felt very cold and about 20 people, including maids and the gardener saw the figure inside and outside the house at all times of the day, and also in the evening, although Captain Despard could not see it. When he learned about the floor boards being nailed over a cavity to hide the jewels, he had them taken up. The cavity was there, but no jewels were found.

There were loud noises in the house and the sound of footsteps in the years between 1884 and 1886. While the family was away on holiday in October 1884 the maids complained of noises in the house. Rosina wrote, however, "As the stair carpets were up, and the house empty, many of these noises were doubtless due to natural causes, though by them attributed to the figure," demonstrating that she would look first for a rational explanation.

The family owned two dogs, a retriever and a Skye Terrier. Both dogs were aware of the ghost, the retriever sometimes being in a state of terror, but the family cat was not affected.

The family lived at GARDEN REACH for about ten years. Rosina became a doctor and qualified with honours at the London School of Medicine in 1895, which is no mean feat today but was quite exceptional at that time so she was obviously not a silly young woman with too vivid an imagination, and it is not easy to understand why her reports of the ghost are questioned.

In the Morton papers, however, Rosina describes a group photograph shown to her from which she picked out a young woman as being very like the ghost. It then transpired that the young woman was, in fact, Imogen's sister whom she had closely resembled.

Remembering this, I was intrigued to receive a letter in September 1982 from Mr. E.S. Lysacht of Monmouth giving me this story about Willey Despard, after he became a Colonel in the Royal Engineers:

"Colonel W.H. Despard, R.E. told this story to my parents and me at tea during a tennis party at his home at St. Briavels in the early 1920s.

He was a very quiet, undramatic person who had been a friend of ours for years, and he only related the experiences as conversation had somehow turned to the supernatural.

He had been at school at Cheltenham College as a day boy, his parents having rented a HOUSE in the Pittville district during that period.

Several members of the family were accustomed to see the ghost of a youngish woman occasionally, and were not in the least perturbed by it. Indeed they came to regard her as almost one of the family, although they did not quite like the possibility of their friends encountering her, as did occasionally happen. It had been known for a friend to offer her a cake during tea, and Billy Despard remembered they would see her outside the french windows of their Georgian drawing room at tea time and someone would say, "Billy shut the window will you, the ghost is outside'.

On leaving school and going into the army his family left Cheltenham. Years later while serving in the army in India he met a family whom he discovered had also lived in Cheltenham at one time. As was customary at the time the family had an album of photographs of their homes and families and these were in due course produced. Amongst them Billy Despard spotted a definite picture of the ghost in a family group. No mention had been made by anyone of a ghost, so Billy said casually, "What a charming looking girl that is."

"Oh yes," was the reply, "That was our family tragedy. She died in Cheltenham and that was one reason why we left. We have since heard rumours that she has haunted the house where she lived ever since."

This was not in accord with the story in the Morton papers in which Rosina described a group photograph including a picture of Imogen's sister, so I wrote to Mr. Lysacht and pointed out the discrepancy. He was rather upset and replied, "Every word of this story is as I heard it myself from Colonel Despard." You must make up your own minds, but stories of a ghost at GARDEN REACH, now named ST. ANNE'S, have continued. It became a boarding school for boys and some of them are said to have been frightened by a ghost. In November 1982 I met an elderly lady named Taylor who had lived in Cheltenham all of her life and she remembered in her childhood two maids had told her mother they had seen a ghost at the school.

Later it became the GLOUCESTER DIOCESAN HOUSE for a short time, and was then turned into flats. When alterations were being made in the 1970s there were reports of workmen being alarmed by a ghost.

There do not seem to have been any recent reports, but noises in flats can always be attributed to other tenants!

Numerous other houses in Cheltenham are reputed to be haunted but the story with which I want to end this book is one of the strangest I have ever been told.

In the late 1960s a new neighbour came to live next door to me and we became friends. In the early days of the last war she had been working as a Sister in a large London hospital, but left to take a commission in Princess Mary's Royal Nursing Service. She enjoyed service life and opted to stay on when the war ended until she reached retirement age.

Discovering my interest in ghosts she told me this story one day:

"My last posting was to Cyprus and one of the first people I bumped into there was a Roman Catholic priest whom I'd first met when I was a newly fledged officer more than 20 years before. I was delighted to see him as he was a man of great integrity whom I had always admired and trusted. He asked where I was going to live after I retired and I told him I had bought a flat near Cheltenham.

"Cheltenham!," He sounded surprised. "I've only been there once and that was when I was a young priest. I've got a very strange memory of that town. I'll tell you about it before you leave.'

He never mentioned it again until three months later when I was preparing to leave, and my goodness the story was strange! I wouldn't have believed it if anyone else had told me, but he was a man whose honesty I would never question.

"When I was young," he told me, "I was instructed to take over the work of an elderly priest in Cheltenham for a short period. I'd never been to the town before, but I was given careful directions to help me find the house, and told the daily woman would leave a cold supper for me.

It was summer time but when I had eaten I thought I might as well go to bed and read even though it was still daylight. I'd no sooner got there though than there was a hammering on the front door. When I went down I found a young man on the step. "Father," he said, "Will you go and see my mother please? She's dying."

"Yes, of course," I said, "But you'll have to wait until I'm dressed and show me the way because I'm a stranger here." I dressed as quickly as I could and we set off together. On the way he told me he was sure his mother would die before morning, and he was anxious she should have the last rites. He was a likeable fellow in his early twenties, with a pleasant open face and a mop of unruly blond hair. I also noticed a small scar near his right eye.

His mother was a widow, he said, and lived alone. His name was Bill and he had served an apprenticeship with a local cabinet maker. When I asked if he was married he said he was not, but he hadn't lived at home for about four years.

It took us about ten minutes to reach a street of little terraced houses and he led me round the back of one of them. We went into the kitchen, which was very quiet and still, and pointing the way to the stairs Bill said, "You'll find my mother in the front room."

As I entered the old fashioned bedroom I could see the woman lying there with her eyes closed looked very frail and ill. On the table by her bedside there was a photograph of Bill, taken I imagine when he was about eighteen. When I moved toward the bed the woman opened her eyes and cried out in alarm, "Go away! Go away! I want none of your sort here!"

I tried to soothe her, but she became very agitated.

"Go away," she kept crying, "Go away and let me die in peace"

"But your son brought me here to see you," I explained.

"I haven't got a son," and she burst into tears.

"Oh, come now," I said, "You've got a fine son. Here he is in this photograph". And I picked it up from the table.

"He's dead," she said, weeping bitterly. "He died four years ago. I've got nobody, that's why I don't believe there's a God, for why should my only son be taken from me?"

"But I've seen your son," I protested, "He came to fetch me. How else would I know you were ill?. I don't belong to Cheltenham; I only arrived here this afternoon."

She looked at me in bewilderment and continued to protest that her son was dead.

"How can you say such things," she demanded, and became more and more agitated. "You're making it all up."

"I'm not making it up I assure you," I said, "Let me tell you what happened."

Then I told her what I've told you; that the young man named Bill had come to fetch me, what he had told me about himself, and what he looked like. When I mentioned the scar she said quietly, "He did that when he fell off his bike going to school."

Somehow that convinced her I was telling the truth. Then she told me how Bill had been killed in an accident four years ago. Until then she had been a practising Catholic, but after his death she had vowed never to go near a church again, or to talk to her priest.

At last, as the tears streamed down her face, we prayed together. I was able to administer the last rites and just before dawn she died, quietly and peacefully.

There was no one downstairs when I left. There were few people at the funeral either because, as a neighbour said, she had no relatives.

Perhaps it would be better to say she had no living relatives. I never saw Bill again, and I don't pretend to understand, but I do know he came to fetch me the night his mother lay dying."

Pittville Park Lake

The Walk

Route: Pittville Pump Room – Pittville Park Boating Lake – Pittville Gates – Pittville Circus and St. Anne's (optional) – Pittville Pump Room.

Distance: $2^1/_4$ miles.

Terrain: Easy walking, virtually all on the flat, along roads and good paths.

Finding Pittville Park: Pittville Park lies to the north of Cheltenham town centre, off Evesham Road (A435). O.S. Landranger Sheet 163 (Cheltenham and Cirencester).

Park and Start: The walk commences from Pittville Pump Room, off the A425, at the northern extremity of Pittville Park. Enter from West Approach Drive. GR 954238. Free parking.

The Route

❑ From the front of the Pump Room nearest the Evesham Road (A435), walk down the grassy slope towards the right-hand extremity of the lake. Pass a children's playground and an aviary on the right.

❑ After crossing the bridge, turn right to go through an underpass beneath Evesham Road. Turn right, cross a footbridge, and follow the edge of a lake on the left. pass a footbridge on the left and continue along the lake margin. The path eventually swings to the left, passing close to an island before returning, between the lake and trees, back to the underpass.

❑ Turn right and continue the walk towards Pittville Gates. Cross Central Cross Drive, passing a tea and coffee house, and keep on to cross Wellington Road to reach the Gates. Notice the Gustav Holst Birthplace Museum to the right across Clarence Road.

❑ To see ST. ANNE'S, turn left along Prestbury Road and second right to reach Pittville Circus. Beyond the Circus, bear left at a fork along Pittville Circus Road. St. Anne's is the first house on the right. Retrace steps to Pittville Circus and cross over and along Wellington Road back into Pittville Park.

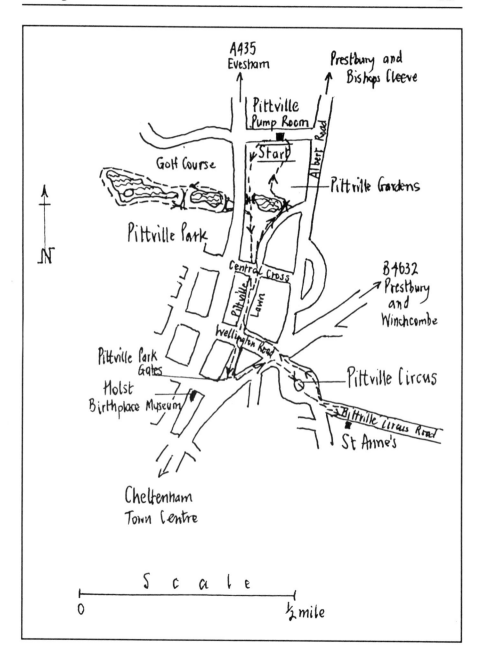

(Those wishing to omit ST. ANNE'S should retrace steps from Pittville Gates as far as Wellington Road).

❑ Turn right back towards the Pump Room. On approaching the ornamental lake once more, go right, and after crossing another bridge, go down the steps on the left and along the lake side for a short distance before walking up the gentle slope back to the Pump Room.

Points of interest

The Pittville area of Cheltenham gets its name from Joseph Pitt (1759-1842), a Gloucestershire-born lawyer and later an MP, who in the early years of the 19th century bought land to the north of the expanding spa with the intention of building a new town.

Although his ambitious scheme was only partly successful, Pitt's 100 acre building estate, with its elegant houses, Pump Room, lake and gardens, plays an important role in Cheltenham's image as a graceful Regency town.

The Pump Room dates from 1830 and was built to the design of John Forbes, a local architect employed by Pitt. It was intended to serve both as a spa and as a centre for social life, but its potential was never fully realised. Since its complete renovation in 1960, however, the Pump Room has taken on a new lease of life and serves as a museum of costume and as a venue for exhibitions and concerts and especially for the staging of events connected with Cheltenham's annual festivals of music and literature.

Cheltenham Spa's supposedly health-giving waters, said to be the only consumable alkaline waters in the British Isles, can still be taken at the Pump Room, although the general opinion of those tasting them is that a little goes a long way!

The delightful little tree-fringed lake, complete with friendly ducks, was created by the damming of Wyman's Brook and the two bridges at either end date from about 1840.

The southern entrance to Pittville Park is through the handsome gates at the top of Winchcombe Street, a reminder that the park was originally a private estate enclosed by railings. On this walk, the gates are reached from Pittville Lawn, a thoroughfare lined on the left by spacious villas and terraces all built between 1832 and 1842.

Those wishing to see the haunted St. Anne's on Pittville Circus Road will need to leave the Park, following the walk instructions, and to retrace steps for a short distance in the vicinity of Pittville Circus. This diversion may not provide a sighting of the ghostly widow but at least it offers a further glimpse of Joseph Pitt's ambitious, if incomplete, project.

Refreshments

Pittville Pump Room, Pittville Park: Open all year – Tuesday/Saturday 11 am/3.30 pm. End of May/September – Sunday 11 am/4.20 pm. (Concerts sometimes restrict access). Lunches and cream teas in summer.

Queen's Hotel, Promenade: Forte 4-star. Accommodation; Restaurant.

Numerous hotels, restaurants and cafes are to be found in or near the town centre.

Nearby Attractions

Pump Room Museum, Pittville Park: Fashion Museum, 1760 to 1930s. Open end of May/September – Tuesday/Saturday – 10 am/4.20 pm. Sunday and Bank Holidays 11 am/4.20 pm. Admission charge.

Holst Birthplace Museum, 4 Clarence Road, Cheltenham: Open Tuesday/Saturday – 10 am/4.20 pm. Closed Bank Holidays. Admission Charge.

Cheltenham Art Gallery & Museum, Clarence Street, Cheltenham: Open Monday/Saturday – 10 am/ 5.20 pm. Closed Bank Holidays.

Imperial Gardens and Montpellier Gardens – nearby Promenade: Cheltenham is noted for its parks and gardens.

Steeplechasing, Prestbury Park: In season. National Hunt Festival in March.

Country Cricket Festival, Cheltenham College: July/August.

Visitor Information Centres

Broadway	Cotswold Court, WR12 7AA. Tel: 0386 852937
Burford	The Brewery, Sheep Street, OX8 4LP. Tel: 099382 3558
Cheltenham	77 The Promenade, GL50 1PP. Tel: 0242 522878
Chipping Campden	Woolstaplers Hall, High Street, GL55 6HB. Tel: 0386 840101
Cirencester	Corn Hall, Market Place, GL57 2NW. Tel: 0285 654180
Evesham	Almonry Museum, Abbey Gate, WR11 4BG. Tel: 0386 446944
Gloucester	St. Michael's Tower, The Cross, GL1 1PD. Tel: 0452 421188
Moreton-in-Marsh	Council Offices, High Street. Tel: 0608 50881
Newent	The Library, High Street. Tel: 0531 822145
Northleach	Cotswold Countryside Collection, GL54 3JN. Tel: 0452 60715
Stow-in-the-Wold	Hollis House, The Square. Tel: 0451 831082
Stroud	Subscription Rooms, George Street, GL5 1AE. Tel: 00453 765 and 768
Tetbury	The Old Court House, Long Street, GL8 8AA. Tel: 0666 502/3
Tewkesbury	64 Barton Street, GL20 5DX. Tel: 0684 295027
Winchcombe	Town Hall, High Street, GL54 5LJ. Tel: 0242 602925

PUBLIC TRANSPORT

British Rail passenger travel information

Gloucester and Cheltenham (Mon-Fri) 0452 529502
Gloucester and Cheltenham (Saturdays) 0452 529503
Gloucester and Cheltenham (Sundays) 0452 529504

Bus and coach services

Castleways (Winchcombe) Ltd – Tel: 0242 602949
Cheltenham & Gloucester Omnibus Co Ltd – Tel: 0242 511655
Perrett & Sons, Shipton Oliffe, Cheltenham – Tel: 0242 820244
Pulham & Sons, Bourton-on-the-Water – Tel: 0451 820369
Stroud Valley Buses, Stroud – Tel: 0453 763421

Bibliography

The Folklore of the Cotswolds   Katherine M. Briggs

Folklore Society   Vol. 69, 1958; Vol.49, 1938

Gloucestershire Through the Ages T A Ryder

Gloucestershire   Arthur Mee

Gloucestershire   Official Guide

Haunted England   Christina Hole

Hidden Gloucestershire   Margaret Sollars

Witches and Sorcerers   Arkon Daraul

Diaries 1915-1918   Lady Cynthia Asquith

Recommended Reading
on Gloucestershire

The Gloucestershire Landscape	H.P.R. Finberg, Hodder & Stoughton, 1975
Portrait of Gloucestershire	T.A. Ryder, Hale 1976
The Gloucestershire Village	Glos.Fed.W.I. Countryside Books, 1987
Hidden Gloucestershire	Margaret Sollars Countryside Books, 1988
Gloucestershire's Green Heritage	Mary Hopkins, Barn Owl Books, 1989
Theme Walks in Gloucestershire	Gordon Ottewell, Thornhill Press, 1989
Gloucestershire	Carole Chester, Christopher Helm, 1990
Gloucestershire Countryside	Gordon Ottewell, Minton & Minton, 1991

Hallowed Ground. Churchyards in Gloucestershire 1993 Hilary Lees, Thornhill Press.

Index

More Books on Gloucestershire and The Cotswolds:

PUB WALKS IN THE COTSWOLDS - Laurence Main

Real Walking with Real Ale! Here are 27 fine walks from 5 to 10 miles. Plenty to suit families and casual walkers, plus a smattering of longer routes. Each walk features a country inn that welcomes walkers and public transport information is included – so there's no need for drivers to miss out! The whole of the county is explored, from sleepy villages to the top of the Broadway Tower. *£6.95*

GLOUCESTERSHIRE HERITAGE WALKS - John Abbott

Here's exercise for both the mind and body: 25 walks that visit Gloucester-shire's historic churches, hill forts, prehistoric sites and present-day places of interest. Super maps and excellent photographs. *£6.95*

CYCLING IN THE COTSWOLDS - Stephen Hill

Safe and interesting routes for riders of all abilities along 500 miles of the most cycle-friendly lanes and tracks in The Cotswolds. Rides range from an easy 11-mile trip to an 80-mile tour. There's even a ride across the county from Oxford to Bath! *£6.95*

Explore the UK with Sigma!

We many more guides to individual towns, plus outdoor activities centred on walking and cycling in the great outdoors throughout England and Wales.

Cycling . . .

CYCLE UK! The essential guide to leisure cycling – Les Lumsdon *(£9.95)*

OFF-BEAT CYCLING & MOUNTAIN BIKING: PEAK DISTRICT – Clive Smith *(£6.95)*

MORE OFF-BEAT CYCLING IN THE PEAK DISTRICT – Clive Smith *(£6.95)*

50 BEST CYCLE RIDES IN CHESHIRE – edited by Graham Beech *(£7.95)*

CYCLING IN THE LAKE DISTRICT – John Wood *(£7.95)*

CYCLING IN SOUTH WALES – Rosemary Evans *(£7.95)*

CYCLING IN NORTH STAFFORDSHIRE – Linda Wain *(£7.95)*

BY-WAY TRAVELS SOUTH OF LONDON – Geoff Marshall *(£7.95)*

Walking . . .

RAMBLES IN NORTH WALES – Roger Redfern

HERITAGE WALKS IN THE PEAK DISTRICT – Clive Price

EAST CHESHIRE WALKS – Graham Beech

WEST CHESHIRE WALKS – Jen Darling

WEST PENNINE WALKS – Mike Cresswell

NEWARK AND SHERWOOD RAMBLES – Malcolm McKenzie

RAMBLES AROUND NOTTINGHAM & DERBY – Keith Taylor

RAMBLES AROUND MANCHESTER – Mike Cresswell

WESTERN LAKELAND RAMBLES – Gordon Brown

**WELSH WALKS: Dolgellau and the Cambrian Coast
– Laurence Main and Morag Perrott**

**WELSH WALKS: Aberystwyth and District
– Laurence Main and Morag Perrott**

– all of these books are currently £6.95 each.

We also publish:

**A fabulous series of 'Pub Walks'
books for just about every popular walking area in the UK,
all featuring access by public transport**

**A new series of investigations into the Supernatural,
Myth and Magic**

– plus many more entertaing and educational books being regularly added to our list. All of our books are available from your local bookshop. In case of difficulty, or to obtain our complete catalogue, please contact:

Sigma Leisure, 1 South Oak Lane, Wilmslow, Cheshire SK9 6AR

Phone: 0625 – 531035   Fax: 0625 – 536800

ACCESS and VISA orders welcome – call our friendly sales staff or use our 24 hour Answerphone service! Most orders are despatched on the day we receive your order – you could be enjoying our books in just a couple of days.